Tolley's
Share Options and Incentives for Directors and Employees

by
Michael Koppel MA FCA
Peter Wolstenholme MA FCA
of Spicer and Pegler

Tolley Publishing Company Limited
A BENN GROUP PUBLICATION

Published by
Tolley Publishing Company Limited
Tolley House
17 Scarbrook Road
Croydon Surrey CR0 1SQ
England
01–686 9141

Photoset by Phoenix Photosetting, Chatham, Kent
Printed in Great Britain by Eyre & Spottiswoode Ltd

ISBN 0 85459 180-X

Contents

	Page
Abbreviations and References	vi
Table of Cases	vi
Table of Statutes	vii
Statutory Instrument	xi
1. Introduction	**1**
2. The General Law	**3**
Share options	3
Introduction	3
The general Schedule E charge	3
Scope of provisions	3
Liability at time of grant	4
Liability after time of grant	5
Exchange of options	7
Schedule E assessment	8
Payment of tax	9
Capital gains tax	10
Information	10
Shares	11
Directors and all employees	11
Acquisition	11
Exemptions	16
Unit trusts	16
Capital growth charge	18
Capital gains tax	18
Information	18
Directors and higher-paid employees	19
Shares issued on favourable terms	19
Stop loss provisions	20
Definitions	21
3. Approved Profit Sharing Schemes	**22**
Outline	22
Who may establish a scheme	24
Scope of schemes	24
Approval procedure	26
Conditions for approval	28
The trust	28
Monetary limit	30
The shares	31
Disposal of shares	33
The participants	35
Tax implications for participants	38
Appropriation of shares	38
Disposal of shares	39
Payments made for rights	41

	Page
Capital receipts	42
Company reconstructions	44
Excess and unauthorised shares	49
Capital gains tax	51
The Schedule E charge	56
The application of PAYE	56
Payments to the trustees	57
The position of the trustees	58
Provision of information	59
Returns	60
Penalties	60
4. Savings-related Share Option Schemes	**61**
Outline	61
Who may establish a scheme	62
Scope of schemes	62
Approval procedure	62
Conditions for approval	64
General	65
Monetary limits	65
Option price	65
Date of exercise of option	66
The shares	69
The participants	70
Transfer of options	73
Income tax and capital gains tax	73
SAYE contracts	74
Information	76
5. Approved Selective Share Option Schemes	**77**
Outline	77
Who may establish a scheme	79
Scope of schemes	79
Approval procedure	79
Conditions for approval	81
General	82
Monetary limit	82
Option price	83
Date of exercise of option	83
The shares	84
The participants	86
Transfer of options	88
Income tax	88
Capital gains tax	91
Information	92
6. Company Law	**93**
Adoption of scheme	93

Page

Disclosure 93
Acquisition of assets by directors 93
Provision of financial assistance 94
Loans to directors 94

7. Investment Committee Guidelines **95**

Appendix **96**
Investment Committee Guidelines 96

Index 103

Abbreviations and References

ABBREVIATIONS

CA	=	Court of Appeal
CA 1985	=	Companies Act 1985
CD	=	Chancery Division
CGTA 1979	=	Capital Gains Tax Act 1979
CIR	=	Commissioners of Inland Revenue
FA	=	Finance Act
HL	=	House of Lords
ICTA 1970	=	Income and Corporation Taxes Act 1970
IHTA 1984	=	Inheritance Tax Act 1984
para	=	paragraph
PAYE	=	Pay As You Earn
s	=	section
SAYE	=	Save As You Earn
Sch	=	Schedule
SI	=	Statutory Instrument
TMA 1970	=	Taxes Management Act 1970
UK	=	United Kingdom

REFERENCES

TC	=	Official Reports of Tax Cases

Table of Cases

Abbott *v* Philbin HL 1960, 39 TC 82	2.1, 2.2, 2.12
Cheatle *v* CIR CD 1982, 56 TC 111	2.42
Heaton *v* Bell HL 1969, 46 TC 211	3.57
Pilkington Bros Ltd *v* CIR HL 1982, 55 TC 705	3.16
Tyrer *v* Smart HL 1978, 52 TC 533	2.42
Weight *v* Salmon HL 1935, 19 TC 174	2.35
Wicks *v* Firth CA 1981, 56 TC 318	2.6

Table of Statutes

1925 Trustee Act
s 34 3.26

1970 Income and Corporation Taxes Act
s 53 3.115
s 186 1.3, 2.2, 2.7, 2.15, 2.34, 2.61, 4.58, 4.59, 5.56, 5.58
(1) 2.3, 2.12
(2) 2.9
(3) 2.13, 2.14
(4) 2.16
(5) 2.19
(5A) 2.16
(5B) 2.16
(6) 2.20
(7) 2.21
(9) 2.3–2.5
(10) 2.3, 2.12
(11) 2.34
(12) 2.33, 5.59
s 224(1) 2.3
s 285(6) 3.56, 4.51, 5.46
s 302 2.45, 2.48, 2.53, 3.42, 3.45, 4.35, 4.41, 5.26, 5.42
s 303(1) 5.47
s 358 2.53
s 526(5) 3.36, 4.37, 5.37
s 533 2.16, 2.37, 2.47, 2.55, 2.71, 4.40, 5.40
s 534 2.45, 3.15, 3.16, 3.36, 3.37, 3.51, 4.10, 4.37, 4.38, 4.47, 5.13, 5.37, 5.38

1970 Taxes Management Act
s 98 2.62, 3.125, 4.63, 5.62

1972 Finance Act
s 75(1) 5.10
s 77 1.3, 4.59, 5.50
(1) 2.7
(2) 2.7
s 79 1.3, 2.52, 2.61
(1) 2.36, 2.41, 2.42
(1A) 2.43
(1B) 2.43
(2) 2.41, 2.44, 2.46, 2.53
(2A) 2.50
(2B) 2.53
(3) 2.41, 2.44
(4) 2.36, 2.56, 2.58, 3.60
(5) 2.57
(5A) 2.36
(5B) 2.36, 2.57
(6) 2.54
(6A) 2.55, 2.57
(7) 2.36
(8) 2.44
(9) 2.60
(10) 2.37
(11) 2.55
Sch 12 1.3
para 3 2.62
para 3A 2.62
para 5 2.62
para 6 2.53
para 7 2.36
Sch 16 para 4(2) 5.47

1973 Finance Act
s 16 3.115
Sch 8 1.3
paras 1–3 2.44
para 4(1) 2.46, 2.50, 2.54
para 5 2.47
para 6(1) 2.48
(2) 2.48
para 7 2.49

1974 Finance Act
s 19(1) 5.10
s 20(2) 2.44
Sch 1 para 9(1) 5.10
para 10(1) 5.10

1976 Finance Act
s 66 — 2.63
(8) — 2.66
s 67 — 1.3, 3.60, 4.55, 5.58
(1) — 2.64
(2) — 2.65
(3) — 2.66
(4) — 2.66
(5) — 2.67
(6) — 2.68, 2.69
(7)–(9) — 2.70
(10) — 2.71
(11) — 2.71
(12) — 2.65
(13) — 2.69

1977 Finance Act
Sch 7 para 1 — 2.5, 3.105

1978 Finance Act
s 53 — 1.4
(1) — 3.17
(3) — 3.60
(4) — 3.27
(5) — 3.61, 3.100
(6) — 3.101, 3.117
(7) — 3.121
(8) — 3.125
s 54 — 1.4
(1) — 3.44, 3.46
(1A) — 3.46
(2) — 3.45
(3) — 3.45, 3.98
(4) — 3.44
(5) — 3.44
(6) — 3.46
(7) — 3.67, 3.68
s 55 — 1.4
(1) — 3.63, 3.67
(2) — 3.67
(3) — 3.67
(4) — 3.72
(5) — 3.72
(6) — 3.64
(7) — 3.66
(8) — 3.70
(9) — 3.72
s 56 — 1.4
(1) — 3.74, 3.76
(2) — 3.75
(3) — 3.75
(4) — 3.77
(5) — 3.79
(6) — 3.76
s 57 — 1.4
(1) — 3.81
(2) — 3.82
(3) — 3.82
(4) — 3.82, 3.83
(5) — 3.84
(6) — 3.87
s 58 — 1.4
(1) — 3.90
(2) — 3.90
(3) — 3.91
(4) — 3.96
(5) — 3.96
(6) — 3.96
(7) — 3.92
s 59 — 1.4
(1) — 3.106
(1A) — 3.118
(2) — 3.107
(3) — 3.107, 3.108
(4) — 3.107, 3.108
(5) — 3.105
(6) — 3.109
(7) — 3.110
s 60 — 1.4
(1) — 3.111
(2) — 3.111, 3.112
(3) — 3.112
(4) — 3.112
s 61 — 1.4
(1) — 3.27, 3.33
(2) — 3.64
(3) — 3.64, 3.71, 3.80
(4) — 3.33
Sch 9 — 1.4
para 1(1) — 3.14, 3.17
(2) — 3.15
(3) — 3.25
(4) — 3.33
(5) — 3.17
para 2(1) — 3.49
(2) — 3.50
(3) — 3.51
(4) — 3.51
para 3(1) — 3.22, 3.43
(2) — 3.21

1978 Finance Act

para 3(3)	3.43
para 4	3.23
para 5	3.36
para 6	3.37
para 7	3.39
para 8	3.42
para 9	3.53
para 10	3.54
para 11(1)	3.55
(2)	3.56
(3)	3.56
para 12	3.27
para 13	3.47
para 14	3.28, 3.29
para 15	3.30
para 16	3.15, 3.36, 3.37, 3.51
para 17	3.36, 3.54, 3.55
para 18	3.14

1979 Capital Gains Tax Act

s 65(5)	3.102
s 137(4)	5.59

1980 Finance Act 4.62

s 46(2)	3.46
(3)	3.44
(5)	3.67, 3.68
(8)	3.118
(10)	3.37
(11)	3.42
(12)	3.56
(13)	3.47
s 47	1.4
(1)	4.54, 4.57
(2)	4.56
s 121	4.63
Sch 10	1.4
para 1(1)	4.9, 4.12, 4.15, 4.47
(1A)	4.47
(2)	4.12
(3)	4.10
para 2	4.16
para 3(1)	4.18
(2)	4.17
para 4	4.19
para 5	4.21
para 6	4.25
para 7	4.28
para 8	4.30–4.32
para 9	4.30
para 10(1)	4.34
para 11	4.27, 4.53
para 12	4.35
para 13(1)	4.21
(2)	4.22
(3)	4.22
para 14	4.23
para 15	4.37
para 16	4.38
para 17	4.39
para 18	4.40
para 19	4.41
para 20	4.45
(1)	4.43
para 21	4.48
para 23(1)	4.50
(2)	4.51
para 24	4.62
para 25	4.63
para 26(1)	4.10, 4.35, 4.37, 4.38, 4.47
(2)	4.51
(3)	4.51
(5)	4.37, 4.50

1981 Finance Act

s 90(3)	4.57

1982 Finance Act

s 40(1)	2.27, 2.28, 2.31, 2.32
(2)	2.32
(3)	2.28
(4)	2.29
(5)	2.29
(6)	2.30
(7)	2.31
(8)	4.35
s 41	2.47, 4.40
s 42(1)	3.74, 3.76
(2)	3.76
s 49(2)–(4)	5.10

1983 Finance Act
s 25(1) 3.33, 3.90
(2) 3.33
(4) 3.49, 3.50
(5) 3.51
(6) 3.22

1984 Finance Act 2.26, 5.1, 5.26
s 38 1.4
(2) 5.50
(3) 5.34, 5.53, 5.59
(4) 5.34, 5.53
(5) 5.50
(6) 5.59
(7) 5.56, 5.58
(8) 5.56
(9) 5.58
(10) 5.62
s 39(1) 4.57
(2) 4.15, 4.47
(3) 4.47
(4) 4.18
(5) 4.22
(6) 4.45
(8) 2.29
s 40(1) 2.53
(2) 2.53
(4) 2.62
(5) 2.53
(6) 2.62
s 41(1) 2.43
Sch 10 1.4
para 1(1) 5.12, 5.15, 5.20
(2) 5.15
(3) 5.13
(4) 5.13
(5) 5.18
para 2(1) 5.22
(2) 5.21
para 3 5.23
para 4(1) 5.43, 5.45
(2) 5.44
(3) 5.46
(4) 5.46
para 5(1) 5.26
(2) 5.28
(3) 5.28
(4) 5.27
(5) 5.29
para 6 5.25
para 7 5.37
para 8 5.38
para 9 5.39
para 10(1) 5.40
(2) 5.41
para 11 5.42
para 12 5.44
(1) 5.49
(2) 5.35
para 13 5.32
para 14 5.61
para 15(1) 5.13, 5.37, 5.38, 5.43
(2) 5.46
(4) 5.37, 5.45

1984 Inheritance Tax Act
s 86 3.119

1985 Companies Act
s 80(1) 6.2
(2) 6.2
s 87(1) 6.2
s 151 6.5
s 152 6.5
s 153(4) 6.5
s 231 6.3
s 235 6.3
s 320(1) 6.4
(2) 6.4
s 323 6.4
s 330 6.6
s 332 6.6
s 425 4.34
ss 428–430 4.34
Sch 5 para 22 6.3
Sch 7 para 2 6.3

1985 Companies Consolidation (Consequential Provisions) Act
Sch 2 4.34

1985 Finance Act
s 45(2) 3.46
(3) 3.67, 3.68

1985 Finance Act

s 45(4)		3.76
Sch 19	para 19(2)	3.103
	(3)	3.103

1986 Finance Act

s 22(1)	3.39
(2)	4.39
(3)	5.39
(4)	3.39, 4.39, 5.39
(5)	3.39
s 23(1)–(3)	3.42, 4.41, 5.42
(4)	2.47, 4.40, 5.41
(5)	3.36, 4.37
s 24(1)	3.14
(2)	3.39
(3)	3.44, 3.46
(4)	3.14
(5)	3.15
s 25(2)	4.16
(3)	4.32
(4)	4.34
(5)	4.35
(6)	4.48
(8)	4.34
(9)	4.34
s 26(1)	2.16
(2)	2.34
(3)	2.36, 2.57
(4)	2.54
(5)	2.55, 2.57
(6)	2.36

Statutory Instrument

1973/334	Income Tax (Employments) Regulations 1973	3.108

Chapter 1

Introduction

1.1 Few aspects of commercial life have had a more chequered history so far as tax is concerned than employee shareholdings.

1.2 There have been successive waves of legislation designed to penalise employee shareholders. Yet from time to time—and particularly in 1972 and from 1978 on—there have also been moves to encourage them, if until recently on a smaller scale than many people might have hoped.

1.3 Shares have long been considered an attractive benefit for a director or senior executive. For this very reason the law contains a highly complex set of provisions designed to ensure that any benefit derived from acquiring and holding shares as a director or employee suffers tax as income rather than as a capital gain. The thrust of these provisions is aimed at various advantages which the director or employee shareholder may enjoy. The provisions deal in particular with

(*a*) share options, which enable the director or employee to acquire shares for less than their real value [*ICTA 1970, s 186; FA 1972, s 77*] (see 2.1 *et seq.* below);

(*b*) shares with potential for capital growth [*FA 1972, s 79, 12 Sch; FA 1973, 8 Sch*] (see 2.36 *et seq.* below);

(*c*) shares conferring special benefits on director or employee shareholders [*FA 1972, s 79*] (see 2.36 *et seq.* below);

(*d*) partly paid shares [*FA 1976, s 67*] (see 2.63 *et seq.* below); and

(*e*) stop loss arrangements designed to ensure that director or employee shareholders are not exposed to the normal risks of share ownership [*FA 1976, s 67*] (see 2.69 *et seq.* below).

1.4 Notwithstanding the provisions to tax employee shareholders, successive governments have considered that, provided stringent conditions were imposed, employee shareholding should be encouraged. In order to ensure that these conditions were met, the concept of the 'approved' employee share scheme was introduced, and this has taken the three following forms

(*a*) profit sharing schemes [*FA 1978, ss 53–61, 9 Sch*];

(*b*) savings-related share option schemes [*FA 1980, s 47, 10 Sch*]; and

(*c*) selective share option schemes [*FA 1984, s 38, 10 Sch*].

These schemes are discussed in detail in Chapters 3, 4 and 5, respectively.

1.5 It is interesting to compare some of the features of the approved employee share schemes, and this is done in the table below.

	Approved profit sharing schemes	Savings-related share option schemes	Approved selective share option schemes
Can the scheme be used to benefit selected employees only?	No	No	Yes
Need the company set up a trust to hold the shares?	Yes	No	No
Are options granted to the participants?	No	Yes	Yes
Are shares acquired by the participants at the start?	Yes	No	No
Do the funds come out of the participant's pocket?	No	Yes	Yes
Is the participant committed to any immediate outlay?	No	Yes	No
Can the scheme be seen as a way of saving, apart from its other advantages?	No	Yes	No

1.6 The implications of company law for employee share schemes are outlined in Chapter 6.

1.7 Finally, the restrictions advocated by institutional investment committees are outlined in Chapter 7.

Chapter 2

The General Law

Share options

Introduction

2.1 Before the introduction of statutory provisions taxing the benefits arising from share options, the position was as follows. Where a share option was granted to a director or employee by reason of his employment, the assessable benefit was restricted to the value of the option at the time of its grant. Any further gain arising on the exercise, assignment or surrender of the option escaped assessment (*Abbott v Philbin HL 1960, 39 TC 82*). By the same token, there was no allowable loss if the option became worthless as a result of a fall in the value of the shares.

2.2 Legislation was subsequently introduced to reverse most of the effects of the decision in *Abbott v Philbin*. The provisions are now to be found in *ICTA 1970, s 186*.

The general Schedule E charge

Scope of provisions

2.3 Subject to 2.5 below, any director or employee is within the scope of this legislation if he acquires a share option by reason of his position as a director or employee, even where the shares under option are not shares in his employer company. The legislation extends both to past and to future directors and employees. [*ICTA 1970, ss 186(1)(9)(a)(10)(c), 224(1)*].

2.4 The provisions are drafted in such a way as to catch the simple avoidance device of granting an option to a third party who subsequently assigns it to a director or employee. Where the option was granted by reason of the assignee's office or employment he is treated as acquiring it as a director or employee, and the provisions discussed in 2.7–2.34 below apply. [*ICTA 1970, s 186(9)(b)*].

2.5 On the other hand the rules apply only where the earnings from the directorship or employment by reason of which the option was granted are assessable under Schedule E, Case I, including cases where a 100% deduction is available under *FA 1977, 7 Sch 1* for long absences abroad. [*ICTA 1970, s 186(9)(a)*].

Where the earnings are assessable under Schedule E, Case II or Case III the normal rules of Schedule E apply. Thus an income tax liability may arise on the grant of the option but not on its exercise, assignment or surrender (see 2.1 above).

2.6 As has been seen, the provisions apply only where an option is granted 'by reason of' an office or employment. There is no definition of the words 'by reason of'. However, the decision of the Court of Appeal in *Wicks v Firth CA 1981, 56 TC 318* (a case which concerned scholarships provided for the children of directors and employees) suggests that a wide interpretation can be put on the words and that a benefit may be provided 'by reason of' a person's office or employment where that is one reason for providing it, even if it is not the sole or main reason.

Liability at time of grant

2.7 Assuming that a share option falls within the scope of *ICTA 1970, s 186*, the tax implications of its grant will depend on the time at which it may be exercised. Where the option is capable of being exercised more than seven years after it is granted, income tax may be charged at the time of grant. [*FA 1972, s 77(1)*]. The liability arises under the general rules of Schedule E (see 2.1 above). In practice, the charge is based on the market value of the shares under option, less the sum of the price payable for them on exercise of the option and the cost of the option itself. Any tax payable in this way is allowed as a deduction from the tax payable on the subsequent exercise, assignment or release of the option. [*FA 1972, s 77(2)*]. But there is no provision for repayment if the option is never exercised, assigned or released or if the amount of tax then payable is less than the amount of tax paid on its grant.

Example 1

2.8 On 1 July 1985 John Smith, a director of John Smith & Sons Limited, was granted an option to subscribe for 10,000 ordinary shares of 50p each in his company at 90p a share. The option, which cost a nominal £1, was exercisable at any time in the next ten years. The market value of the shares on 1 July 1985 was £10,000. A Schedule E assessment will be made for 1985/86 as follows.

	£	£
Market value of shares at 1.7.85		10,000
Less: Cost of option	1	
Exercise price	9,000	9,001
Assessable under Sch E, 1985/86		£999
Income tax at, say, 50%		£499.50

2.9 Where an option is not capable of being exercised more than seven years after it is granted, no income tax will be charged on its grant, since in this case the legislation specifically excludes any charge that might arise under the general rules of Schedule E or under any other provision. [*ICTA 1970, s 186(2)*].

2.10 If liability is to be avoided when an option is granted, there must be no circumstances in which the option can be exercised more than seven years after grant. This condition might be infringed unwittingly. Suppose, for instance, that the normal expiry date of an option is the seventh anniversary of its grant, but that the holder's personal representatives are permitted to exercise the option within six months of his death, if that occurs before the option has expired. In such a case there are circumstances where the option could be exercised more than seven years after grant, and therefore the rule in 2.9 above will not apply. Instead, income tax may be charged on the grant of the option as explained in 2.7 above.

2.11 It may also be vital to identify correctly the date on which an option is granted. This is governed by the normal rules of the law of contract.

(*a*) Where a company offers a director or employee an option and he accepts, supporting his acceptance with (probably nominal) consideration, the date of his acceptance marks the date when the contract is completed and therefore the date on which the option is granted. If he accepts the offer by post, the contract will be completed at the time when he posts his acceptance, and not on the later date when the acceptance is received.

(*b*) On the other hand, where the company merely invites a director or employee to apply for an option, the date on which the option is granted is the date when the company accepts the offer made by the employee. Unless the company grants the option using a deed, the director or employee will have to support his offer with (probably nominal) consideration.

Where (*a*) above is in point, care must be taken to ensure that the option can in no circumstances be exercised more than seven years after the date of acceptance of the offer.

Liability after time of grant

2.12 Regardless of whether there is an income tax charge on the grant of an option, a liability will arise on its exercise, assignment or release. This is the most important way in which the legislation reverses the effect of the decision in *Abbott v Philbin* (see 2.1 above). The word 'release' here includes an agreement to any restriction of the exercise of the option. [*ICTA 1970, s 186(1),(10)(a)*].

2.13 If the option is exercised, the gain chargeable to income tax is the excess of the market value of the shares at the time of exercise over the sum of the price payable for them under the option and the cost of the option itself. The market value of the shares at the time of their allotment, if later than the exercise of the option, is not relevant. There is a proviso to the effect that the performance of the director's or employee's duties is not to count as consideration given for the grant of the option. [*ICTA 1970, s 186(3)(a)*].

2.14 If the option is assigned or released, the gain chargeable to income tax is the excess of the consideration the director or employee gets for giving up the option over the consideration he gave for it. The market value of the shares plays no part in the calculation, even if the assignment or release is not an arm's length transaction. There is a proviso to the effect that the performance of the director's or employee's duties is not to count as consideration given for the grant of the option. [*ICTA 1970, s 186(3)(b)*].

Example 2

2.15 The facts are the same as in Example 1 above. John Smith exercised his option on 1 July 1989 when the market value of the shares was £20,000. The amount assessable under *ICTA 1970, s 186* will be computed as follows.

	£	£
Market value of shares at 1.7.89		20,000
Less: Cost of option	1	
Exercise price	9,000	9,001
Assessable under Sch E, 1989/90		£10,999
Income tax at, say, 60%		6,599.40
Less: Income tax payable on grant of option		499.50
		£6,099.90

2.16 In the following further circumstances a liability can arise after the time of grant.

(*a*) Any money or money's worth received for

(i) omitting, or undertaking to omit, to exercise an option; or

(ii) granting, or undertaking to grant, to a third party a right to acquire any of the shares or an interest in them,

is taxable as if it were received for the assignment or release of the option. Where tax is so charged, there is nothing to stop a subsequent liability arising, e.g. where a third party acquires shares by exercising an option. No part of the cost of the option deducted in calculating the first tax charge can be deducted in calculating any subsequent liability. (This is simply a provision to prevent double relief from being obtained.) [*ICTA 1970, s 186(5A)(5B); FA 1986, s 26(1)*].

(*b*) Subject to 2.19 below, a director or employee is chargeable where an option granted by reason of his employment is exercised by a third party if

- (i) the option was granted to that third party; or
- (ii) the third party acquired the option otherwise than by way of an arm's length bargain; or
- (iii) the director or employee and the third party are connected persons (as defined in *ICTA 1970, s 533*) when the option is exercised.

Where the third party acquired the option by assignment, the assessable gain on his exercise of it is reduced by any gain made by a previous holder. [*ICTA 1970, s 186(4)*].

2.17 The provisions described in 2.16 above are intended to frustrate attempts by directors and employees to avoid liability by agreeing to forgo their rights or arranging for an option to be exercised by a third party. It will be seen that, where an option is exercised by a third party, an income tax liability may fall not on the third party but on the director or employee, who may not have, and may not have access to, the funds to meet that liability. Care should be taken to avoid this position.

Example 3

2.18 John Brown & Sons Limited grants an option for £1 to Tom Jones by reason of John Brown's position as a director of the company. Jones subsequently sells the option to John Brown's sister Anne Other, for £1,000 (its then market value). Anne Other eventually exercises the option realising a gain of £1,500, being the difference between the price she paid for the shares and their market value.

John Brown will be chargeable on

(*a*) the gain of £999 (£1,000−£1) realised by Tom Jones on assignment of the option; and

(*b*) the net gain of £500 (£1,500−(£1+£999)) realised by his sister.

2.19 Where a director or employee is divested of an option by operation of law, e.g. on his bankruptcy, the rules in 2.16 above do not apply. Instead, the person in whom the option is vested, e.g. the trustee in bankruptcy, is assessed under Schedule D, Case VI if he exercises the option. [*ICTA 1970, s 186(5)*].

Exchange of options

2.20 There is what might be described as a form of rollover where the consideration for the assignment or release of an option consists of or includes another option. In such a case, for income tax purposes

(*a*) the new option is not treated as consideration for the assignment or release of the old; and

(*b*) the assignment or release of the old option is not treated as consideration for the grant of the new.

Instead, the consideration given for the grant of the old option is attributed to the new option. Where the consideration for the assignment or release of the old option includes assets other than the new option, the consideration given for the grant of the old option must be apportioned, and only the appropriate proportion is attributed to the new option. Thus an exchange of options where no other consideration passes gives rise to no income tax liability. On the other hand, the Schedule E provisions apply to the new option exactly as they did to the old, so that there is no possibility of arguing, say, that the individual obtained the new option as an existing option holder and not as a director or employee. [*ICTA 1970, s 186(6)*].

2.21 The 'rollover' provisions also apply where there is an indirect exchange of options by means of two or more transactions involving two or more directors or employees, and

(*a*) a director or employee ceases to hold one option; and

(*b*) he or a connected person acquires another option, whether or not from the person to whom the first option was assigned.

[*ICTA 1970, s 186(7)*].

2.22 Where the new option can be exercised more than seven years after it is granted, the 'rollover' provisions do not prevent the normal income tax charge from arising at the time of grant. For the purpose of calculating this charge, the cost of the new option will in practice be taken as the cost (or the appropriate proportion of the cost) of the old option (see 2.20 above).

2.23 Furthermore, the 'rollover' provisions apply for the purposes of income tax only. Thus a chargeable gain may well arise on the assignment or release of one option in return for the grant of another.

Schedule E assessment

2.24 The gains assessed under Schedule E do not appear strictly speaking to constitute emoluments assessable under any of the three Cases of that Schedule. In practice, however, they seem to be treated as such, with the result that, where an option is exercised by a individual working abroad, the gain may escape tax because he is not resident in the UK or because the 100% deduction is available.

Payment of tax

2.25 A person who realises a 'gain' on the exercise of an option finds that he is out of pocket, having invested in the shares, but at the same time faces an income tax bill. Provisions originally introduced in 1982, and amended in 1984, go some way towards softening the blow.

2.26 A person who is liable to income tax on the exercise of an option granted before 6 April 1984 may elect to pay the tax by five equal instalments if certain conditions are met (see 2.27–2.32 below). In the case of options granted after 5 April 1984, the right to pay income tax by instalments is withdrawn. This is intended to encourage companies to adopt schemes capable of obtaining approval under *FA 1984* (see Chapter 5). In such schemes, no income tax liability will normally arise.

2.27 It should be noted that the election to pay by instalments cannot be made where a liability arises on the assignment or release of an option; the election can be made only if an option is actually exercised. [*FA 1982, s 40(1)(a)*].

2.28 Any taxpayer wishing to avail himself of the right to pay by instalments must elect to do so in writing to the inspector within 60 days of the end of the year of assessment in which he exercises the option—a very short time limit. [*FA 1982, s 40(1)(d)(3)*].

2.29 Where an election is made the tax is payable in five equal instalments due as follows

(*a*) the first, 14 days after the tax is demanded under the PAYE regulations;

(*b*) the fifth, on the last day of the fifth year of assessment after that in which the option is exercised; and

(*c*) the second, third and fourth at equal intervals between (*a*) and (*b*).

[*FA 1982, s 40(4); FA 1984, s 39(8)*].

If the first instalment is not due until after the fifth instalment would normally be due (e.g. as a result of delay in valuing shares which in turn delays the first demand) all instalments become due on that later date. [*FA 1982, s 40(5); FA 1984, s 39(8)*].

2.30 Tax deferred by an election may be paid early and will become due immediately if the taxpayer becomes bankrupt. [*FA 1982, s 40(6)*].

2.31 Payment by instalments can be claimed only if, as a result of the exercise of the option, income tax in excess of £250 is collectable under the PAYE regulations following an assessment for the year in which the option is exercised. For this purpose, the amount of tax on the gain is to be calculated by taking the gain as the top slice of income, subject to any other provisions for determining the top slice of a taxpayer's income. [*FA 1982, s 40(1)(c)(7)*].

2.32 The right to pay by instalments generally exists only if the price paid for the shares on the exercise of an option

(*a*) is not less than the market value of shares of that class (as calculated for capital gains tax purposes) when the option was granted; or

(*b*) in the case of an option granted before 6 April 1982, is not less than 90% of the market value of shares of that class when the option was granted.

The taxpayer can elect to pay by instalments even if shares are acquired for less than the minimum value laid down in (*a*) or (*b*) above, provided that the only reason for this is a reduction in the market value of shares of that class resulting from a reorganisation of the share capital of the company (e.g. a bonus issue) after the option was granted. [*FA 1982, s 40(1)(b)(2)*].

Capital gains tax

2.33 Where an income tax liability arises under the provisions discussed in 2.13 above, the amount assessed under Schedule E is added to the cost of the shares for the purpose of future capital gains tax computations, thus eliminating double taxation. [*ICTA 1970, s 186(12)*].

Information

2.34 Where a company

(*a*) grants an option in respect of which tax may become chargeable under *ICTA 1970, s 186*; or

(*b*) allots or transfers any shares on the exercise of such an option; or

(*c*) receives written notice of the assignment of such an option; or

(*d*) provides any benefit, in money or money's worth: for the assignment or release (in whole or in part) of such an option; or in connection with an omission (or undertaking to omit) to exercise such an option; or in connection with the grant of (or undertaking to grant) a right to acquire shares (or an interest in shares),

it must send the inspector particulars in writing within thirty days of the end of the tax year in which the event in question occurs. [*ICTA 1970, s 186(11); FA 1986, s 26(2)*].

Shares

Directors and all employees

Acquisition

2.35 Any director or employee who acquires shares as part of his emoluments is potentially assessable under the general rules of Schedule E. If he acquires such shares without having to pay the full market value for them, the difference will be taxed as a benefit in kind (*Weight v Salmon HL 1935, 19 TC 174*).

2.36 In addition, there are rules which apply only where shares are acquired by the holder of an office or employment the earnings from which are assessed under Schedule E, Case I. [*FA 1972, s 79(1), 12 Sch 7*]. These rules state that any person who acquires shares, or an interest in shares, in pursuance of a right conferred on him or opportunity offered to him as a director or employee and not in pursuance of an offer to the public may be charged under Schedule E on any growth in the value of the shares over a period of time (see 2.54 below). [*FA 1972, s 79(4)*]. Furthermore, such a person may be taxed under Schedule E on any benefit he receives as owner of the shares if that benefit is not received by the majority of ordinary shareholders who did not acquire their shares as directors or employees. An example would be a bonus issue confined to employee shareholders. [*FA 1972, s 79(7)*].

If, after 18 March 1986, such a person acquires additional shares by virtue of his original holding, all the shares are treated as if they were a single holding acquired at the time of acquisition of the original holding; and the market value of the original holding is apportioned on a pro rata basis. Where the additional shares were acquired by way of a rights issue, the cost of the rights is treated as additional consideration for the holding (see 2.57(*a*) below). [*FA 1972, s 79(5A)(5B); FA 1986, s 26(3)(6)*].

2.37 A director or employee is treated as acquiring any shares which are in fact acquired by a person connected with him (as defined in *ICTA 1970, s 533*) if that person acquires the shares as a result of his connection with the director or employee. This means that the 'capital growth' and 'exceptional benefit' charges noted in 2.36 above fall not on the connected person but on the director or employee, who may not have, and may not have access to, the funds to meet them. [*FA 1972, s 79(10)*]. This is comparable with the rule where a share option is exercised by a third party (see 2.17 above). Care should be taken to avoid this position.

2.38 As has been seen (see 2.36 above), the rules apply where a director or employee acquires 'shares or an interest in shares'. It is considered that an individual who becomes the beneficial owner of shares acquires 'shares' even if they are held by a nominee. On the other hand, a beneficiary under a trust, other than a bare trust, acquires an 'interest in shares'. A share option is not treated as an 'interest in shares' for the purposes of these provisions.

2.39 Not every director or employee who acquires shares in his company is within the scope of these provisions. There are cases where such a director or employee acquires the shares as proprietor or investor, e.g. where he incorporates a business formerly carried on by him alone or in partnership. However, the dividing line between acquisition as investor and acquisition as director or employee can be a fine one.

Exemptions

2.40 There are a number of cases in which the provisions do not apply even where an individual acquires shares or an interest in shares as a director or employee. The table below lists these cases and should enable the reader to tell at a glance whether a particular exemption is available on the acquisition of shares, on the acquisition of an interest in shares, or both, and whether it exempts only from the 'capital growth' charge or extends to the 'exceptional benefit' charge as well. The exemptions are discussed in more detail in 2.41–2.53 below.

Circumstance	Exempts		From	
	Shares	Interests in shares	'Capital growth' charge	'Exceptional benefit' charge
Acquisition before 6 April 1972 (see 2.41(*a*))	Yes	Yes	Yes	Yes
Acquisition before 27 March 1974 under approved scheme (see 2.41(*b*))	Yes	Yes	Yes	Yes
Acquisition in an offer to the public (see 2.42)	Yes	Yes	Yes	Yes
Acquisition under a 'discount offer' (see 2.43)	Yes	Yes	Yes	Yes
Acquisition under a profit sharing scheme (see 2.44)	Yes	Yes	Yes	Yes
Acquisition of 'normal' shares (see 2.45–2.52)	Yes	No	Yes	No
Acquisition of units (see 2.53)	No	Yes	Yes	No

2.41 No liability will arise under these provisions where shares or interests in shares were acquired

(*a*) before 6 April 1972 [*FA 1972, s 79(1)*]; or

(*b*) before 27 March 1974 under an approved share incentive or share option scheme, provided that the director or employee meets certain conditions. [*FA 1972, s 79(2)(a)(3)(a)*].

2.42 Shares or interests in shares acquired in an offer to the public are not within the scope of the provisions (unless the director or employee enjoys preferential treatment, e.g. under the 'pink form' procedure, as in *Tyrer v Smart HL 1978, 52 TC 533*). [*FA 1972, s 79(1)*].

The decision in *Cheatle v CIR CD 1982, 56 TC 111* shows that the expression 'in an offer to the public' refers to an invitation made to the public generally to subscribe for shares in response to a prospectus or to purchase them from an issuing house to which the whole issue has been allotted. Thus the exemption for shares acquired in an offer to the public will not normally apply where special arrangements have been made for employees.

2.43 Shares or interests in shares acquired under an offer to directors and employees as such (a 'discount offer') are treated as acquired in an offer to the public, and therefore escape the 'capital growth' and 'exceptional benefit' charges, if

(i) the discount offer is made to directors and employees in conjunction with an offer to the public, the only difference being that the directors and employees are allowed a discount on the subscription price;

(ii) the directors and employees are assessable under Schedule E on the discount; and

(iii) at least 75% of the total number of shares issued go to the public, and not to directors or employees.

[*FA 1972, s 79(1A)(1B); FA 1984, s 41(1)*].

2.44 Shares and interests in shares acquired under profit sharing schemes are exempt from the 'capital growth' and 'exceptional benefit' charges. [*FA 1972, s 79(2)(b)(3)(b)(8)*]. However, where the provisions of a profit sharing scheme have been made or altered after 22 March 1973, the exemption will apply only if the following conditions relating to the shares and to the participants are met.

(*a*) The shares must be quoted, or, failing that, must be shares in a company which is not under the control of any other company. They must not be subject to restrictions which may enable their holder to benefit from capital growth after acquisition, and they must not be capable of being exchanged for or converted into shares which are subject to such restrictions, whether by one transaction or by a series of transactions. In other words, the shares must be such that they are unlikely to undergo exceptional capital growth.

(*b*) The scheme must allow everyone who has been a full-time director or employee of the company for not less than five years, whose earnings are assessed under Schedule E, Case I and who is twenty-five or over, to acquire shares, or interests in shares, of the same class on similar terms. In other words, the scheme must not be selective.

[*FA 1973, 8 Sch 1–3; FA 1974, s 20(2)*].

2.45 'Normal' shares are exempt from the 'capital growth' charge. Shares are treated as 'normal' if either of the two following sets of conditions is fulfilled immediately after acquisition.

(i) The shares are not subject to 'restrictions', and the majority of shares of the same class, disregarding any held by an associated company (as defined in *ICTA 1970, s 302*), are not held by persons who acquired them as directors or employees.

(ii) The shares are not subject to restrictions and the majority of shares of the same class, disregarding any held by an associated company, have been acquired by directors or employees who together are able, as holders of those shares, to control the company within the meaning of *ICTA 1970, s 534.*

2.46 For the purposes of 2.45 above, shares are treated as subject to restrictions if they are capable of being converted into, or exchanged for, shares which are subject to restrictions. [*FA 1972, s 79(2)(c); FA 1973, 8 Sch 4(1)*].

2.47 The term 'restriction' includes any contract, agreement, arrangement, or condition which

(*a*) limits a person's freedom to dispose of his shares or of any interest in them; or

(*b*) limits his freedom to exercise any right conferred by those shares; or

(*c*) might make such a disposal or exercise disadvantageous to him or to any person connected with him.

'Connected person' here has the meaning given in *ICTA 1970, s 533*. [*FA 1973, 8 Sch 5*].

However, restrictions similar to those in the Stock Exchange 'Model Code for Securities Transactions by Directors of Listed Companies' issued in November 1984 will be ignored. [*FA 1982, s 41; FA 1986, s 23(4)*].

2.48 It will be seen from 2.47 above that shares are prima facie subject to a restriction where they are used as security for a loan. However, the use of shares as security will not count as a restriction provided that the loan is not made, arranged, guaranteed or in any way facilitated by (*a*) the employer company; or

(*b*) an associated company as defined in *ICTA 1970, s 302*; or

(*c*) in the case of a close company, a person having a material interest in the company.

Even where the lender falls within (*a*), (*b*), or (*c*) above, the use of shares as security will not count as a restriction if making personal loans is an ordinary part of his business, e.g. if the lender happens to be a banker. [*FA 1973, 8 Sch 6(1)(2)*].

2.49 There is one other important limitation of the wide meaning of the word 'restriction'. Shares are not treated as subject to restrictions merely because a director or employee is required to sell them to a specific person at not more than market value in the event of his ceasing to be a director or employee. [*FA 1973, 8 Sch 7*].

2.50 Not every 'restriction' attaching to shares is detrimental. The restrictions which bring shares within the scope of the 'capital growth' charge are restrictions which

(*a*) do not apply to all shares of the same class; or

(*b*) are, or may be, temporary; or,

(*c*) are dependent on the shares being, or ceasing to be, held by directors or employees (but disregarding any provision in the company's articles requiring a director or employee to dispose of his shares on ceasing to work for the company. [*FA 1972, s 79(2A); FA 1973, 8 Sch 4(1)*].

2.51 While one or other of the exemptions in 2.45 above will take many employee shareholdings out of the net, there are certain common circumstances in which those exemptions are not likely to apply.

(*a*) One such case is where a director or employee of a subsidiary acquires shares in his own company. If he (or he and his fellow directors and employees) are the only shareholders apart from the parent company, the exemption in 2.45(*a*) above will not apply, because all shares not held by the parent company are held by directors or employees. On the other hand, the exemption in 2.45(*b*) above will not apply, because the director and employee shareholders do not control the company. Apparently shares in a subsidiary are treated unfavourably because it is considered too easy to manipulate their value for the benefit of director or employee shareholders.

(*b*) A second case is where directors and employees of an employee-controlled company hold both 'A' (voting) and 'B' (non-voting) shares. The exemption in 2.45(*b*) above may apply to the 'A' shares, but will not apply to the 'B' shares since the employees cannot control the company as holders of those shares.

Formerly, one possible solution to these problems was to have a bonus issue or rights issue. The new shares acquired in such an issue were arguably outside the scope of the 'capital growth' charge, while the value of the original shares was diluted, possibly eliminating all liability. Now, however, additional shares acquired after 18 March 1986 are treated as part of the original holding (see 2.36 above). An alternative solution was to impose an artificial restriction such as a short-term embargo on voting the shares. When this embargo ceased, the 'capital growth' charge would be triggered but the taxpayer would probably suffer little or no tax penalty. This kind of device will no longer work, because now the lifting of all restrictions triggers the 'capital growth' charge only if other conditions are satisfied; see 2.54(*c*) below. Failing this the charge will not be triggered until the shares are disposed of or until seven years after acquisition, whichever is the earlier.

2.52 The aim of the provisions is to tax the capital growth of shares which are subject to restrictions when issued and therefore have exceptional potential to rise in value when those restrictions are lifted. However, a liability can arise in many unexpected circumstances, and any acquisition of shares by a director must be carefully vetted to ensure it will not fall foul of *FA 1972, s 79.*

Unit trusts

2.53 The 'capital growth' charge will not apply where, after 5 April 1984, a director or employee acquires units in an authorised unit trust approved by the Board for this purpose. [*FA 1972, s 79(2)(bb); FA 1984, s 40(1)*].

Shares in the employing company or in an associated company (as defined in *ICTA 1970, s 302*) must not constitute more than 10% by value of the authorised unit trust's portfolio at any time when the director or employee has a right to acquire units or holds units already acquired. However, if such shares exceed the 10% limit for a continuous period of less than one month, e.g. because of fluctuations in share values, this will be ignored. [*FA 1972, s 79(2B); FA 1984, s 40(2)*].

For the purpose of this exemption 'authorised unit trust' has the same meaning as in *ICTA 1970, s 358*. [*FA 1972, 12 Sch 6; FA 1984, s 40(5)*].

Capital growth charge

2.54 The period of time over which the growth in the value of the shares is measured for the purposes of the 'capital growth' charge begins with acquisition and ends (subject to 2.55 below) with the first of the following

(*a*) the seventh anniversary of acquisition;

(*b*) the date on which the director or employee ceases to have a beneficial interest in the shares; and (*c*) if shares were acquired, the date on which, by reason of the shares ceasing to be subject to restrictions as defined in 2.47–2.50 above, either of the sets of conditions described in 2.45 above would be satisfied if the shares had been acquired then.

[*FA 1972, s 79(6); FA 1973, 8 Sch 4(1); FA 1986, s 26(4)*].

2.55 A disposal of shares to a connected person (as defined in *ICTA 1970, s 533*) is deemed not to bring beneficial ownership to an end. [*FA 1972, s 79(11)*]. Thus a gift of shares by a director or employee to, say, his wife, will not trigger the 'capital growth' charge.

If a person ceases to have a beneficial interest in any shares but acquires others in circumstances constituting a reorganisation for capital gains tax, the new holding is equated with the original one for the purposes of the 'capital growth' charge, with the result that the charge is not triggered then. [*FA 1972, s 79(6A); FA 1986, s 26(5)*].

Both these forms of 'rollover' may benefit the Revenue more than the taxpayer, or they will defer the 'capital growth' charge with the possible result that a greater amount of growth will have occurred.

2.56 The 'capital growth' charge is calculated as the difference between two market values, and the calculation is therefore unaffected by the question whether the shares are acquired or disposed of at market value or not. [*FA 1972, s 79(4)*].

2.57 The 'capital growth' calculation may need to be adjusted in the following cases.

(*a*) Where additional consideration becomes payable under the terms on which the acquisition of the shares was made (e.g. because part of the acquisition price was deferred and contingent on results), that additional consideration is deducted from the assessable gain. [*FA 1972, s 79(5)(a)*].

(*b*) Where, in accordance with the terms on which the acquisition of shares was made, the shares are subsequently disposed of for a consideration which is less than their market value at the time of disposal, the amount assessed is the difference between disposal proceeds and market value at the time of acquisition. [*FA 1972, s 79(5)(b)*].

(*c*) Where consideration is given for additional shares acquired as described in 2.36 above, it is treated as additional consideration within (*a*) above. [*FA 1972, s 79(5B); FA 1986, s 26(3)*].

(*d*) Where consideration is given for a new holding acquired in a reorganisation within 2.55 above, it is treated as additional consideration within (*a*) above. Where consideration is received in such a reorganisation, no tax is charged then, but the consideration is added to the market value of the new holding when the 'capital growth' charge is triggered. [*FA 1972, s 79(6A); FA 1986, s 26(5)*].

2.58 When the capital growth has been calculated it is treated as earned income assessable under Schedule E for the year of assessment in which the measurement period ends. There is no relief for the fact that the whole of the gain falls in one tax year. [*FA 1972, s 79(4)*].

Example 4

2.59 The facts are the same as in Examples 1 and 2 above. When John Smith exercises his option on 1 July 1989, he needs to borrow in order to take up his shares. A bank loan, guaranteed by John Smith & Sons Ltd, is secured on the shares. John Smith is able to repay the loan on 1 July 1991 after receiving a legacy. There are no other restrictions attaching to the shares.

The repayment of the loan will trigger the 'capital growth' charge and the assessment will be computed as follows.

	£
Market value of shares at 1.7.91	30,000
" " " " " 1.7.89	20,000
Assessable under Sch E, 1991/92	£10,000

Capital gains tax

2.60 Amounts assessed under the 'capital growth' and 'exceptional benefit' provisions are added to the cost of shares in any subsequent capital gains tax computation. [*FA 1972, s 79(9)*].

Example 5

2.61 The facts are the same as in Examples 1, 2 and 4 above. The cost of John Smith's shares for capital gains tax purposes is as follows.

	£
Cost of option	1
" " shares	9,000
Assessed under *ICTA 1970, s 186* (see 2.15 above)	10,999
" " *FA 1972, s 79* (see 2.59 above)	10,000
Total cost for capital gains tax	£30,000

Information

2.62 Where a person acquires shares, or an interest in shares, which may fall within the provisions now under discussion, the company must send the inspector particulars in writing within thirty days of the end of the tax year in question.

The Board can also require the managers or trustees of an approved unit trust of the kind described in 2.53 above to provide information to establish whether the shareholding condition in 2.53 above is fulfilled and to enable the Board to determine the tax liability of an employee who acquires units. [*FA 1972, 12 Sch 3, 3A; FA 1984, s 40(4)*]. Penalties can be imposed for failure to supply the information required. [*TMA 1970, s 98; FA 1972, 12 Sch 5; FA 1984, s 40(6)*].

Directors and higher-paid employees

Shares issued on favourable terms

2.63 Where a company issues shares to a director or employee for a consideration which is less than the market value of the shares on the date of issue the difference between the market value and the consideration paid is taxable as an emolument under the general rules of Schedule E (see 2.35 above).

Where a director or higher-paid employee acquires fully paid shares and the consideration for the shares is wholly or partly left outstanding as a debt, the 'cheap loan' provisions may apply to that debt. [*FA 1976, s 66*].

Where, however, shares are issued at market value but only part of the price is payable on issue, neither of the foregoing situations exists, because

(i) taking into account the liability to pay calls in future the consideration is not less than the market value; and

(ii) until a call is made, no consideration is outstanding as a debt.

2.64 Therefore provisions exist to deal with cases where, after 6 April 1976, a director or higher-paid employee, or a person who is about to become a director or higher-paid employee, acquires nil or partly paid shares. The provisions also apply where such shares are acquired by a connected person. [*FA 1976, s 67(1)*].

2.65 The provisions are stated to apply where the person acquires shares 'at an under-value' in pursuance of a right or opportunity available by reason of the employment.

Shares are acquired 'at an under-value' if the amount (if any) paid for them at the time of acquisition is less than the market value of fully paid up shares of the same class. However, any amount which is otherwise taxable under Schedule E is excluded. [*FA 1976, s 67(2)(12)*]. Therefore as a simple issue at an under-value would be taxed under other provisions (see 2.35 above), this provision applies only to the amount unpaid on the shares.

2.66 If the provisions apply there is deemed to be an interest-free loan equal to the market value of an equal number of fully paid up shares of the same class less the amount paid for the shares at the time of acquisition and any amount taxable under Schedule E. [*FA 1976, s 67(3)(4)*]. Income tax is therefore chargeable on the equivalent of interest at the official rate, unless the interest on an actual loan would have qualified for relief. [*FA 1976, s 66(8)*]. The payment of a future call on the shares is deemed to be a repayment of an equal amount of the loan. [*FA 1976, s 67(4)(b)*].

2.67 The loan comes to an end when

(*a*) the whole amount is discharged by payments for the shares; or

(*b*) the employee, or person connected with him, is released from the obligation to pay any balance outstanding; or

(*c*) the shares are disposed of in such a way that neither the employee nor any person connected with him has any longer any beneficial interest in the shares; or

(*d*) the employee himself dies.

[*FA 1976, s 67(5)*].

2.68 A benefit in kind arises on the termination of the loan (whether or not the employment continues) except where the loan is discharged in full or the employee dies. The amount of the benefit is the amount of the notional loan outstanding at the time of the termination. [*FA 1976, s 67(6)*]. Thus if the shares go down in value after issue but, whether because of the terms of issue or for some other reason, the employee does not have to pay any further calls, he is taxed on the loss he would otherwise have made. There appears to be an anomaly in that if an employee sells his partly paid shares at full value subject to the liability to future calls which is transferred with the shares he is taxed as if he had been forgiven a loan (and therefore received a benefit under these provisions).

2.69 In order to avoid double taxation, the amount chargeable as a Schedule E benefit under *section 67(6)* (see 2.68 above) is allowed as an expense of acquisition of the shares in calculating the capital gain or loss on the disposal. [*FA 1976, s 67(13)*].

Stop loss provisions

2.70 Where shares which were acquired after 6 April 1976 by a director or higher-paid employee (or a person connected with him) in pursuance of a right or opportunity available by reason of the employment are subsequently sold, surrendered or otherwise disposed of for a consideration which exceeds the then market value, the excess is chargeable to income tax under Schedule E. This applies whether or not the original issue was at an under-value, and is a rule designed to tax the benefit which might arise from a stop loss provision if, between acquisition and sale, the value of the shares drops but on sale the employee is protected against loss. He is taxed on the loss he would have made as if he had received income. However, if the disposal occurs after the death of the employee no such benefit arises. If the employee does not die but ceases to be employed, the benefit is chargeable as if the employment had not ceased. [*FA 1976, s 67(7)–(9)*].

Definitions

2.71 The acquisition and disposal of shares includes the acquisition and disposal of an interest in shares, including an interest in the proceeds of sale of part of the shares but excluding a share option. [*FA 1976, s 67(10)*].

The term 'shares' includes stock and other securities, whether secured by a charge on the company's assets or not. [*FA 1976, s 67(11)(a)*].

'Connected persons' are defined as in *ICTA 1970, s 533*. [*FA 1976, s 67(11)*].

'Market value' is given the capital gains tax definition. Difficulty is bound to arise in valuing unquoted shares. [*FA 1976, s 67(11)(d)*].

Chapter 3

Approved Profit Sharing Schemes

Outline

3.1 An approved profit sharing scheme works as follows. The company sets up and funds a trust for the benefit of its directors and employees. This trust acquires ordinary shares either in the company itself or in a related company (the 'scheme shares'). The trustees hold the scheme shares for the benefit of those directors and employees who are members of the scheme (the 'participants'). Eventually, the scheme shares are transferred to the participants and registered in their own names.

3.2 First, the company must set up a trust for the benefit of directors and employees. The trust deed will contain the rules that the trustees have to follow. The rules must require that all benefits arising from the ownership of scheme shares are passed on to the participants for whom those shares are held. The trustees must also be required to keep full records so that they can provide both the participants and the Inland Revenue with any information that is needed.

3.3 The trustees must acquire scheme shares and appropriate them to the participants. There is a limit on the value of the shares that can be appropriated to any one participant in any one tax year. The limit is normally 10% of salary, with a ceiling of £5,000. But those earning less than £12,500 are entitled to a yearly appropriation of £1,250. The figures quoted are maxima. The rules of the scheme may provide for smaller appropriation.

3.4 The scheme shares must form part of the equity of

(*a*) the employing company; or

(*b*) its parent company; or

(*c*) in some cases, a member of a consortium owning the employing company or its parent; or

(*d*) a company controlling such a consortium member.

3.5 The shares may be quoted or unquoted, but shares in an unquoted subsidiary do not qualify unless the ultimate parent company is quoted. This means that the shares of a trading subsidiary in an unquoted group cannot be used as scheme shares.

3.6 Generally speaking, once shares have been appropriated to a participant, they must not be sold for two years.

3.7 Approved profit sharing schemes must be open to everybody who has completed a qualifying period of service. This qualifying period must not exceed five years. It is not possible to use a scheme of this type to benefit selected directors and employees only, and all the participants must benefit from the scheme on similar terms. This does not preclude variations depending on length of service or level of remuneration, but it is not permissible to favour, say, directors and senior executives on an arbitrary basis.

3.8 There is no income tax liability when shares are appropriated to a participant, but if those shares are sold within five years of appropriation there will be an income tax penalty. This penalty is on a sliding scale; it reduces the longer the shares are held. To get the full benefit of the scheme, the participant must retain his shares for five years. If he sells them after that, he will only have to pay capital gains tax—or no tax at all if the gain is within the annual exemption.

3.9 There are also provisions to tax sums of cash derived from the shares during the first five years after appropriation, e.g. a cash element in a paper-for-paper takeover of the company.

3.10 Broadly speaking, the normal capital gains tax rules apply to transactions involving scheme shares.

3.11 The PAYE procedures are adapted to collect any income tax which becomes payable under the profit sharing provisions.

3.12 The trust in which the scheme shares are held is funded by payments from the company. These payments are tax deductible so long as the money is used to acquire shares within nine months of the end of the accounting period. The Inland Revenue can extend this deadline at their discretion.

3.13 It will be seen from what has been said above that an approved profit sharing scheme offers a number of advantages. Among them are the following

(*a*) No contribution is required from directors and employees participating in the scheme.

(*b*) The benefits the scheme offers are completely free of income tax etc. in the hands of the participants (provided that certain conditions are met).

(*c*) The cost of funding the scheme is tax deductible for the employer company.

(*d*) The payments made by the company need not reduce the working capital of the business.

On the other hand, directors and employees must accept that the benefits of participation in a profit sharing scheme are long term, and that they will need to wait at least five years before realising their gains, if they wish to enjoy those benefits to the full.

Who may establish a scheme

3.14 Any body corporate may establish a profit sharing scheme and obtain approval under these provisions. [*FA 1978, 9 Sch 1(1)*]. The body establishing the scheme need not be incorporated or resident in the UK. And if it is incorporated in the UK, it need not be a company formed under the Companies Acts. It may, for instance, be a chartered company. However, it must be in a position to establish a scheme complying with the rules described in this chapter. It must be able, inter alia, to issue to its directors and employees shares satisfying the conditions described in 3.36–3.43 below. And, unless at least some of the individuals participating in the scheme are within the UK tax net, there will be little point in going to the trouble of obtaining Revenue approval.

There are specific provisions enabling workers' co-operatives to introduce approved profit sharing schemes. For this purpose a 'workers' co-operative' is a registered industrial and provident society, as defined by *ICTA 1970, s 340*, which is a co-operative society and has employee members only. The arrangements necessary for vesting in the trustees the shares issued under the profit sharing scheme will not prejudice a co-operative's eligibility for continued registration under the industrial and provident societies legislation. [*FA 1978, 9 Sch 18; FA 1986, s 24(1)(4)(5)*]. The special rules applying to profit sharing schemes run by workers' co-operatives are referred to in 3.39, 3.44 and 3.46 below.

Scope of schemes

3.15 In many cases, the benefits of a profit sharing scheme will be restricted to the directors and employees of the company which has established it. But where the company running such a scheme is the parent company of a group, the scheme may extend to the directors and employees of any of its subsidiaries. A scheme for a parent company and its subsidiaries is known as a 'group scheme', and any company which is included in the scheme (there is no need to include every company in the group) is referred to as a 'participating company'. For this purpose, a subsidiary is any company over which the parent has control. 'Control' has the meaning given in *ICTA 1970, s 534*. [*FA 1978, 9 Sch 1(2), 16*]. It is possible that a parent company which is in turn under the control of another company could establish a group scheme to extend to the directors and employees of its subsidiaries; see 3.16 below. But this scheme could not extend to the directors and employees of its holding company.

Example 1

3.16 The following diagram represents the structure of the A plc group. The percentages quoted reflect voting power in the companies concerned.

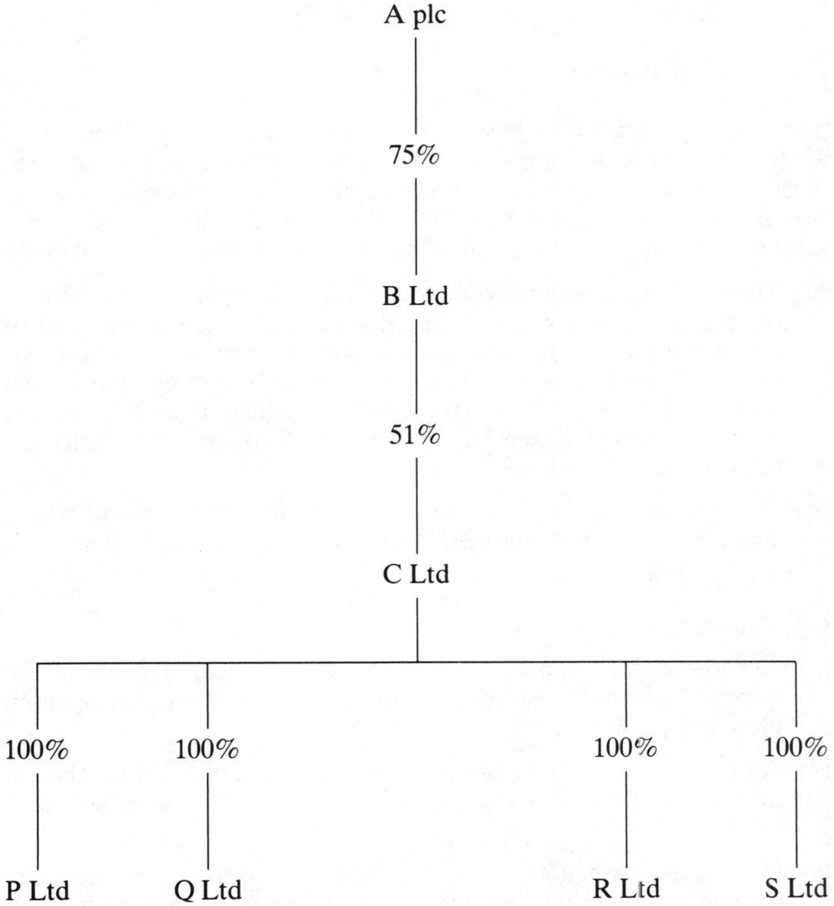

(*a*) It is considered that A plc controls every company in the group within the meaning of *ICTA 1970, s 534* (*Pilkington Bros Ltd v CIR HL 1982, 55 TC 705*). On this assumption, it can establish a group scheme to extend to each of those companies.

(*b*) In the light of Lord Bridge's remarks in the *Pilkington* case, it may be doubted whether B Ltd or C Ltd can be said to control any other company in the group. If this is correct, each of the companies in the above diagram other than A plc can establish a scheme for the benefit of its own directors and employees, but none of those schemes can extend to the directors and employees of any other company.

(*c*) It is hoped that the Revenue would in practice adopt a more liberal interpretation of 'control'. If they did, B Ltd could establish a group scheme to extend to C Ltd and its subsidiaries, and C Ltd could establish a group scheme to extend to its subsidiaries.

It should be noted that a scheme established by a subsidiary may have to use A plc's shares. This could prove an obstacle to the establishment of such a scheme (see 3.37–3.38 below).

Approval procedure

3.17 A company which has established a profit sharing scheme may apply to the Board for approval. The application must be in writing and must contain such information and be supported by such evidence as the Board may require. [*FA 1978, s 53(1), 9 Sch 1(1)(5)*]. There is no special form of application, but the following information should be provided.

(*a*) The name and registered office of the company which has established the scheme, the tax district to which it makes its returns and its reference number in that district. This information will also be required for the company whose shares are to be appropriated, if that is not the company which has established the scheme, and, in the case of a 'group scheme' (see 3.15 above), for all companies to which the scheme extends.

(*b*) The memorandum and articles of association of the company whose shares are to be appropriated, and any relevant amendments.

(*c*) The trust instrument.

(*d*) The scheme rules.

(*e*) A copy of the proposed contract (see 3.44 below) between the company which has established the scheme and every participant in the scheme.

(*f*) A declaration, by the company which has established the scheme, that the scheme shares will satisfy the conditions set out in 3.36–3.43 below.

(*g*) If the shares which are to be acquired and appropriated under the scheme are not shares in the company which has established the scheme, a further declaration specifying which of the conditions in 3.36–3.43 below is met, and how.

(*h*) Any other documents which will be issued to participants and/or shareholders in connection with the scheme, e.g. the announcement of the scheme to shareholders and employees, and statements to be provided to participants following an appropriation of shares.

3.18 Applications for approval should be addressed to: Inland Revenue, Technical Division (Employee Share Schemes), Somerset House, London WC2R 1LB.

3.19 The legislation envisages that approval will be obtained only after a scheme has been drawn up and adopted by a company. There is no provision for the company to obtain advance confirmation that the terms of a scheme which it proposes to establish will qualify. A common procedure is to adopt a scheme and then amend the rules if need be in order to obtain approval. In addition, it is understood that the Technical Division (Employee Share Schemes) is prepared to comment informally on draft documentation and to discuss particular points of difficulty in advance of a formal application for approval.

3.20 The Board do not have any discretion with regard to the approval of profit sharing schemes. They are obliged to approve a scheme provided that it meets the requirements listed at 3.24 below and that it does not include 'features . . . which are neither essential nor reasonably incidental' to its purpose of providing shares for directors and employees. A provision allowing the payment of cash in lieu of shares would violate this condition.

3.21 Any alteration to an approved scheme, however minor, must itself be approved by the Board, or the scheme as a whole will automatically lose its approved status from the date the alteration is adopted. [*FA 1978, 9 Sch 3(2)*]. This is an important point which can all too easily be overlooked in practice. It is therefore advisable to include in the rules of the scheme a provision that no alteration is to be made without the Board's prior approval.

3.22 Even where there is no alteration to a scheme the Board's approval may be withdrawn if

(*a*) a participant is in breach of his obligations in connection with the disposal of his shares (see 3.44 and 3.46 below); or

(*b*) there is a contravention of any of the rules concerning the running of the scheme, of the scheme itself, or of the terms of the trust in which the scheme shares are held (see 3.25–3.57 below); or

(*c*) any shares of a class some of which have been appropriated to participants are treated differently from other shares of the same class (see 3.43 below); or

(*d*) the requirements as to the eligibility of employees to participate in the scheme are no longer met (see 3.49 below); or

(*e*) the trustees, the company or, in the case of a group scheme (see 3.15 above), any participating company, fail(s) to provide information required by the Board (see 3.121 below).

[*FA 1978, 9 Sch 3(1); FA 1983, s 25(6)*].

3.23 Where the Board refuses to approve a scheme, refuses to approve an alteration, or withdraws an approval previously given, the company may appeal to the Special Commissioners within 30 days of notification. [*FA 1978, 9 Sch 4*]. It should be noted that the participants, who are likely to be most seriously affected by the Board's decision, do not have any right of appeal.

Conditions for approval

3.24 If it is to obtain approval a scheme must satisfy a number of conditions. These are discussed below under five main headings:

(*a*) conditions relating to the trust (see 3.25–3.32 below);

(*b*) conditions imposing monetary limits on an individual's participation in the scheme (see 3.33–3.35 below);

(*c*) conditions relating to the shares (see 3.36–3.43 below);

(*d*) conditions relating to disposal of the shares (see 3.44–3.47 below); and

(*e*) conditions relating to the participants (see 3.48–3.57 below).

The trust

3.25 It is a condition of approval of a profit sharing scheme that it provides for trustees resident in the UK whose duty it is

(*a*) to acquire scheme shares with money provided by the company (or, in the case of a group scheme, by any participating company);

(*b*) to appropriate those shares to individuals participating in the scheme and eligible to benefit; and

(*c*) to deal with those shares in accordance with a trust which contains the specific provisions described in 3.27–3.32 below and which is governed by the law of a part of the UK. [*FA 1978, 9 Sch 1(3)*].

3.26 The trustees may be individuals or companies or a combination of the two.

There is no rule about the number of trustees. While a company could act as sole trustee, an individual could not, because the legislation refers to the trustees as 'a body of persons'. As the trust will be one of pure personalty, the statutory maximum of four trustees laid down by *Trustee Act 1925, s 34* will not apply.

The requirement that the trustees be resident in the UK seems strictly speaking to apply to each of the trustees separately, with the result that all the trustees must be resident in the UK, not merely a majority of them. However, it is understood that the Board will approve a scheme if only one of the trustees is UK resident.

3.27 The trust instrument must require the trustees to give a participant notice, as soon as practicable after they have appropriated shares to him, of the number and description of those shares and of their 'initial market value'. [*FA 1978, 9 Sch 12*]. The 'initial market value' is the market value of the shares on the date of appropriation, unless the Board and the trustees agree in writing to take the market value at some earlier date.

[*FA 1978, s 53(4)*]. 'Market value' is defined in the same way as for capital gains tax. [*FA 1978, s 61(1)*]. Where the shares are not quoted, the initial market value will have to be agreed with the Inland Revenue's Share Valuation Division. This may take time, and accordingly the trustees should notify participants of the number and description of shares appropriated to them while undertaking to advise them of the initial market value as soon as possible.

3.28 The trust instrument must also require the trustees to account to each participant for any money or money's worth that comes into their hands in respect of his shares, subject to their obligations under the PAYE rules discussed in 3.106–3.110 below. This requirement covers sale proceeds, dividends etc., but not new shares arising in a company reconstruction or amalgamation. [*FA 1978, 9 Sch 14(a)*].

3.29 The trustees must be required not to act without the instructions of the participant, or other person in whom the beneficial interest in his shares is vested, in connection with any rights issue. [*FA 1978, 9 Sch 14(b)*]. This rule seems harmless enough, but it could mean that, if a participant wished to take up his rights but failed to instruct the trustees to acquire them, he would derive no benefit from the issue at all. It is understood, however, that a scheme can be approved if it contains a standing instruction for the acquisition of rights.

3.30 The trustees must also be required to maintain any records necessary to enable them to account for income tax under PAYE and to inform the participants of any facts relevant to the determination of their tax liability. [*FA 1978, 9 Sch 15*].

3.31 The facts which are considered relevant to the determination of such a tax liability include

(*a*) the past history of the shares disposed of, including dates of appropriation and details of subsequent capital reorganisations, company reconstructions, etc.;

(*b*) the 'locked-in value' of the shares (see 3.67 below);

(*c*) the proceeds of disposal;

(*d*) the market value of the shares at the time of disposal if different from the proceeds of disposal; and

(*e*) the amount of income tax, if any, deducted under the PAYE provisions.

There seems to be no statutory obligation to provide information to a participant's successors in title, such as his personal representatives, even where a liability arises, say, on a participant's death. This could happen where the participant held 'excess' or 'unauthorised' shares (see 3.89–3.98 below).

3.32 The trust instrument must impose restrictions on the disposal of a participant's shares by the trustees. These restrictions are discussed in 3.47 below. They mirror the restrictions on disposal imposed on the participants.

Monetary limit

3.33 The scheme must provide that the total initial market value of the shares appropriated to any one employee in any one year of assessment is not to exceed the 'relevant amount'. This is the greater of

(*a*) £1,250; and

(*b*) 10% of salary, subject to an overriding maximum of £5,000.

The 10% limit in (*b*) above is calculated on salary paid in the current or the preceding year of assessment, whichever is the higher. In this context, 'salary' means earnings from the office or employment entitling the individual to participate in the scheme. Only earnings from which income tax has to be deducted under PAYE may be taken into account. Benefits in kind and reimbursed expenses are ignored. [*FA 1978, s 61(1)(4), 9 Sch 1(4); FA 1983, s 25(1)(2)*]. Earnings qualifying for the 100% deduction for long absences abroad also appear strictly speaking to be excluded from this calculation. It is hard to reconcile this with the requirement that all directors and employees who decide to participate in the scheme (and all Schedule E, Case I employees must be eligible to participate) should do so on similar terms. It is to be hoped that the Revenue would adopt a more liberal approach to overseas earnings in practice.

3.34 Where one is dealing with quoted shares the initial market value will normally be easy to determine. But in other cases the initial market value of shares will not be so readily ascertainable and therefore the limits could be unintentionally exceeded. This would lead to some of the shares being treated as excess shares (see 3.89 below). The possible solutions are to agree a valuation with the Share Valuation Division before appropriation, or to allow a wide margin for error when appropriating shares to participants.

Example 2

3.35 John Smith's income as a director of Smith & Jones plc is as follows.

		1984/85		1985/86
		£		£
Salary		20,000		24,000
Bonus paid in year		10,000		5,000
Car benefit	750		825	
Fuel benefit	750		825	
Golf club subscription	120	1,620	150	1,800
		£31,620		£30,800

His maximum entitlement in 1985/86 is 10% of (£20,000 + £10,000) = £3,000

The shares

3.36 The scheme shares must form part of the ordinary share capital of

(i) the company which established the scheme; or

(ii) a company having control of the company which established the scheme; or

(iii) a company which is a member of a consortium owning either the company in (i) or the company in (ii) and which itself owns beneficially not less than 15% of the consortium company in question; or

(iv) a company which has control of the consortium member in (iii).

[*FA 1978, 9 Sch 5*].

'Control' has the meaning given in *ICTA 1970, s 534*. [*FA 1978, 9 Sch 16*]. A company is a member of a consortium owning another company if it is one of a number of companies owning between them not less than 75% of the other company's ordinary share capital and each owning not less than 5% of that ordinary share capital. [*FA 1978, 9 Sch 17; FA 1986, s 23(5)*]. 'Ordinary share capital' has the meaning given in *ICTA 1970, s 526(5)*, and therefore includes participating preference shares.

3.37 The scheme shares must be

(*a*) quoted shares; or

(*b*) unquoted shares in a company which is not under the control of any other company; or

(*c*) unquoted shares in a company which is under the control of a quoted company (other than a quoted company which is, or would if resident in the UK be, a close company).

'Control' has the meaning given in *ICTA 1970, s 534*. [*FA 1978, 9 Sch 6, 16; FA 1980, s 46(10)*].

Thus a scheme for, say, directors and employees of a trading subsidiary in an unquoted group is likely to rely on the shares of the parent company. The shares of the trading subsidiary cannot be scheme shares. It is apparently considered that the profits of a subsidiary can too easily be manipulated to the benefit or detriment of the employee shareholders. It will be seen that the link between the growth in the value of the scheme shares and the profitability of the company for which a participant works may be a very tenuous one. This seems inconsistent with the role of a profit sharing scheme as an incentive to improve the profitability of the participant's own company.

Example 3

3.38 Assume that the facts are the same as in Example 1 above, and that A plc is not a close company.

3.39 *Approved Profit Sharing Schemes*

S Ltd has established an approved profit sharing scheme.

If A plc is a quoted company, the scheme shares can be shares in S Ltd, A plc, B Ltd or C Ltd.

If A plc is not a quoted company, the scheme shares must be shares in A plc itself.

3.39 The shares must be fully paid up, must not be redeemable except in the case of a workers' co-operative, and must not be subject to any restrictions not attaching to all shares of the same class, with the following exception.

It is permissible for the company's articles of association to require that all shares held by directors and employees be sold on cessation of employment. However, the articles must require that the shares be sold for cash, and must prescribe the terms of sale. What is more, these terms must apply to all holders of shares of the same class, not just to directors and employees. In other words, the terms of sale must form part of general disposal provisions. Except in the case of a workers' co-operative, such disposal provisions must not require a participant to sell his beneficial interest in shares before the release date (see 3.46 below) if the ownership of the shares has not been transferred to him. [*FA 1978, 9 Sch 7; FA 1986, s 22(1)(4)(5), 24(2)*].

3.40 The profit sharing legislation includes no definition of the word 'restriction' but it is considered that the term should be interpreted as including any contract or agreement which

(*a*) limits a person's freedom to dispose of his shares, of any interest in them or of the proceeds of their sale; or

(*b*) limits his freedom to exercise any right conferred by those shares; or

(*c*) might make such a disposal or exercise disadvantageous to him.

3.41 The restrictions in question are restrictions attaching to the shares themselves. They do not include personal restrictions imposed on a particular owner of shares, like the restrictions on disposal which must be imposed on all participants as a condition of the approval of a profit sharing scheme (see 3.44 below).

3.42 If at the time when the trustees acquire the scheme shares the company has more than one class of ordinary share capital, the majority of the shares of the class to which the scheme shares belong must *either* be 'employee-control shares' *or* be held by persons other than

(*a*) persons who acquired their shares in pursuance of a right conferred on them or an opportunity afforded to them as directors or employees; or

(*b*) trustees for such shareholders (e.g. the trustees of an approved profit sharing scheme); or (*c*) in the case of unquoted shares, any company which controls the company whose shares are scheme shares or of which that company is an associated company (as defined in *ICTA 1970, s 302*).

'Employee-control shares' are shares held by present or former directors or employees of the company or of a company it controls who together are able, as holders of those shares, to control the company in question.

[*FA 1978, 9 Sch 8; FA 1980, s 46(11); FA 1986, s 23(1)–(3)*].

3.43 The Board may withdraw approval if shares of a class some of which have been appropriated to participants in the scheme are treated differently from other shares of the same class in any respect, and in particular in respect of

(*a*) dividends (but see below); or

(*b*) repayment; or

(*c*) restrictions attaching to shares; or

(*d*) any offer of substituted or additional shares, securities or rights in respect of shares.

The requirement with regard to dividends (see (*a*) above) does not mean that newly issued shares must rank for the next dividend on the same basis as shares of the same class already in issue. [*FA 1978, 9 Sch 3(1)(c)(3)*].

Disposal of shares

3.44 No profit sharing scheme may be approved unless the Board are satisfied that every participant is bound in contract with the company which has established the scheme (whether under the terms of the scheme or otherwise) to permit his shares to remain in the hands of the trustees for the 'period of retention' and not to assign, charge or otherwise dispose of the shares during that period except in one of three permitted ways (see 3.45 below). This holds good in a group scheme even where the participant is not a director or employee of the company running the scheme. The 'period of retention' normally ends two years after the date of appropriation of the shares to the participant. But if within those two years the participant

(i) resigns from his job by reason of injury or disability; or

(ii) is made redundant; or

(iii) reaches pensionable age (65 for men and 60 for women); or

(iv) dies; or

(v) in the case of redeemable shares in a workers' co-operative, ceases to be employed by, or by a subsidiary of, the co-operative,

the 'period of retention' ends with whichever of those events occurs first. It should be noted that, in the case of a group scheme, the period of retention does not come to an end under (i) or (ii) above so long as the participant remains a director or employee of any participating company. [*FA 1978, s 54(1)(a)(b)(4)(5); FA 1980, s 46(3); FA 1986, s 24(3)*].

3.45 As stated above, a participant may dispose of his shares during the period of retention only in one of three ways.

(i) He may accept new shares in a company reconstruction or amalgamation where 'rollover' is available for capital gains tax purposes so that his new holding is equated with his original shares.

(ii) He may accept an offer wholly or partly in cash provided that it is a general offer to shareholders and is conditional in the first instance on the offeror obtaining control of the company. In this case, 'control' has the wide meaning given in *ICTA 1970, s 302*.

(iii) He may agree to a compromise, arrangement or scheme so long as this is not restricted to shares held by employees or by scheme participants but will apply to all the shares of the class in question or to all the shares of that class held by a particular type of shareholder. [*FA 1978, s 54(2)*].

If during the period of retention, the participant assigns, charges or disposes of his shares in any other way, the result is that the shares concerned are treated as 'unauthorised' shares and the participant's tax liability is computed accordingly (see 3.89 *et seq.* below). [*FA 1978, s 54(3)*].

3.46 After the end of the period of retention a participant is permitted more freedom to deal with his shares, but certain restrictions apply until the 'release date', which falls five years after the date of appropriation of the shares. [*FA 1978, s 54(6); FA 1985, s 45(2)*]. In addition to disposing of those shares in any of the ways described in 3.45 above, a participant may, before the release date

(i) direct the trustees to sell his shares for cash, provided that the sale is for the best price that can be obtained in the market at the time; or

(ii) sell his beneficial interest in his shares to the trustees for cash, for a price that would be acceptable in the third party sale described in (i) above; or

(iii) direct the trustees to transfer the legal ownership of his shares to him, on payment to the trustees of a sum equal to basic rate income tax on the 'appropriate percentage' of the 'locked-in value' (see 3.67 below) of the shares at the time. This payment is credited against the participant's income tax liability resulting from the disposal of the shares by the trustees (see 3.63 below). No such payment is required when the trustees transfer legal ownership of shares to a participant's personal representatives.

The effect of these rules is to ensure that, where shares are disposed of before the release date, tax cannot be avoided by giving them away or selling them at an undervalue. [*FA 1978, s 54(1)(c)(d)(1A); FA 1980, s 46(2)*].

After the end of the period of retention, redeemable shares in a workers' co-operative may also be disposed of by redemption. [*FA 1978, s 54(1)(d); FA 1986, s 24(3)*].

3.47 The trustees are subject to restrictions which reflect those imposed on the participant. The trust instrument must prohibit the trustees from disposing of the shares during the period of retention except in one of the three ways described in 3.45 above. The trustees must also be prohibited from disposing of the shares after the end of the period of retention but before the release date except

(*a*) at the direction of the participant or of the person in whom his shares have vested, such as his trustee in bankruptcy or his personal representatives; and

(*b*) in a way which involves no breach of the rules discussed in 3.46 above.

[*FA 1978, 9 Sch 13; FA 1980, s 46(13)*].

The participants

3.48 The conditions relating to the participants have the effect of dividing a company's directors and employees into three categories

(*a*) those who must be eligible to participate under the rules of any approved scheme (see 3.49–3.52 below);

(*b*) those who must be excluded from benefit by the rules of any approved scheme (see 3.53–3.56 below); and

(*c*) those whose inclusion or exclusion is optional and may vary from scheme to scheme (see 3.57 below).

3.49 With the exceptions noted in 3.53 to 3.56 below, the scheme must be open on similar terms to every full-time director or employee of the company – and, in the case of a group scheme, of any participating company – whose earnings are taxable under Schedule E, Case I and who has completed a qualifying period of service of five years. [*FA 1978, 9 Sch 2(1); FA 1983, s 25(4)*]. There is no definition of the term 'full-time director or employee', but it is understood that the Revenue regard a director or employee as 'full-time' if he spends at least 25 hours a week working for his company.

3.50 There are provisions designed to counter attempts to restrict the benefits of profit sharing schemes to chosen personnel. Thus not only must the scheme be open on similar terms to all directors and employees who satisfy the criteria in 3.49 above, but all those who decide to participate, even if they do not satisfy those criteria but are merely permitted to participate under the rules of a particular scheme (see 3.57 below), must in fact do so on similar terms. This does not mean on identical terms, as the number of shares appropriated to participants may depend on salary level, length of service and other similar factors. [*FA 1978, 9 Sch 2(2); FA 1983, s 25(A)*]. While it is not clear exactly what other factors may be taken into account in determining the level of an individual's participation in addition to salary and length of service, the profitability of the company for which he works would clearly merit consideration. On the other hand, arbitrary discrimination is not permissible.

3.51 The Board must also be satisfied that the scheme does not discourage any employees or former employees from participating if they fulfil the requirements in 3.49 above. And, where the company is a member of a group, the scheme must not concentrate its benefits wholly or mainly on the directors or highest paid employees of companies in the group. This rule is intended to prevent the use of a single company to employ all the group's directors and senior executives with the object of establishing a profit sharing scheme for their benefit alone. For this purpose, a group comprises a parent company and any companies over which it has control. 'Control' has the meaning given in *ICTA 1970, s 534*. [*FA 1978, 9 Sch 2(3)(4), 16; FA 1983, s 25(5)*].

Example 4

3.52 Assume that the facts are the same as in Example 1 above.

Assume also that A plc employs all directors in the group and seconds them to their respective companies but has no other employees.

Under the general rules (see 3.15 above), it would be permissible for A plc to establish a profit sharing scheme for the benefit of its employees alone. However, such a scheme would not qualify for approval in the light of 3.51 above.

3.53 The rules of the scheme must provide that nobody other than a director or employee of the company, or of a participating company in the case of a group scheme, is eligible to benefit, except that a former director or employee may have shares appropriated to him up to eighteen months after his resignation. [*FA 1978, 9 Sch 9*].

3.54 A director or employee must not be eligible to have shares appropriated to him under the scheme in any year of assessment in which he has already benefited under another approved profit sharing scheme run by

(i) the same company; or

(ii) a company which controls, is controlled by, or is under the control of the same company as, that company; or

(iii) a member of a consortium owning that company; or

(iv) a company part-owned by that company as a member of a consortium.

'Consortium' has the same meaning as in 3.36 above. [*FA 1978, 9 Sch 10, 17*].

Provided that the monetary limits are not exceeded (see 3.33–3.35 above), an individual may have shares appropriated to him more than once in the same year of assessment under the same scheme or under two unrelated schemes. He may also participate in both forms of approved share option scheme as well as an approved profit sharing scheme, even if all three schemes are run by the same company.

3.55 An individual must not be eligible to benefit under a scheme if he or his associates have, or in the preceding twelve months have had, a 'material interest' in a close company which is

(*a*) the company whose shares are to be scheme shares; or

(*b*) a company controlling that company or a member of a consortium owning that company.

In determining whether a person has a material interest in a company, the interests of his associates must be taken into account.

'Consortium' has the same meaning as in 3.36 above.

[*FA 1978, 9 Sch 11(1)(17)*].

3.56 The close company legislation applies for the purpose of the provision in 3.55 above with the following amendments

(*a*) No other participant under the profit sharing scheme is treated as an associate unless he and his relatives own, or could acquire as a result of the working of the scheme, more than 25% of the company's ordinary share capital. [*FA 1978, 9 Sch 11(3)(a)(c); FA 1980, s 46(12)*]. Under the normal close company rules, the figure of 5% would have to be substituted for 25%.

(*b*) A person is only treated as having a 'material interest' in a company if he owns or can control more than 25% of the ordinary share capital or if more than 25% of the company's distributable income could be apportioned to him. [*ICTA 1970, s 285(6); FA 1978, 9 Sch 11(3)(a)(b)*]. Again, the figure of 5% would have to be substituted for 25% under the normal close company rules.

(*c*) The term 'close company' here includes any company not resident in the UK which would be close if it were so resident and any company which would be close but for the fact that some of its shares are quoted on a recognised stock exchange. [*FA 1978, 9 Sch 11(2)(3)(a)*].

3.57 It should be noted that the rules discussed above merely specify a minimum class of participant. It is permissible to include others, e.g. those with less than five years' qualifying service, those who do not work full-time, those whose earnings are assessed under Schedule E, Case II or III, or those who have resigned within the preceding eighteen months.

However, if people in these categories decide to participate, they must do so on similar terms to all other participants (see 3.50 above). On the other hand, there is no need for all eligible directors and employees to participate in a scheme, although there seems little point in not participating if that would mean forgoing the benefits the scheme can offer. It might seem attractive for a company to provide an alternative in the form of, say, a cash bonus. This would undoubtedly be taxable under Schedule E, but some employees might still prefer to take cash rather than shares. But great care would have to be taken in establishing the arrangements. If there were a formal 'cash alternative' it would be open to the Revenue to claim that a Schedule E liability arises on general principles (*Heaton v Bell HL 1969, 46 TC 211*) when shares are appropriated to a participant, notwithstanding the exemption provided for approved profit sharing schemes (see 3.60 below).

Tax implications for participants

3.58 The tax treatment of the participants is considered below under seven main headings

(*a*) appropriation of shares (see 3.59–3.62 below);

(*b*) disposal of shares (see 3.63–3.73 below);

(*c*) capital receipts (see 3.74–3.80 below);

(*d*) company reconstructions in general (see 3.81–3.88 below);

(*e*) excess and unauthorised shares (see 3.89–3.98 below);

(*f*) capital gains tax (see 3.99–3.104 below); and

(*g*) the Schedule E charge (see 3.105 below).

Appropriation of shares

3.59 In practice, the rules of an approved profit sharing scheme will need to contain detailed provisions dealing with the appropriation of shares to participants, covering such matters as how, when and by whom entitlement is to be determined. However, the legislation lays down no specific rules on these matters.

3.60 At the time of the appropriation of shares to a participant there is no liability on him under the general rules of Schedule E. Were it not for this exemption the market value of the shares would be assessable as a benefit in kind. Furthermore the provisions of *FA 1972, s 79(4)* (see 2.36 *et seq*. above) (which tax the capital growth of certain employee shareholdings over a period of time) and of *FA 1976, s 67* (see 2.64 *et seq*. above) (which treat an employee who acquires shares not fully paid as having the benefit of an interest-free loan) do not apply where shares are appropriated under an approved profit sharing scheme. [*FA 1978, s 53(3)*].

3.61 When the trustees appropriate shares to a participant, he may or may not become the beneficial owner of those shares depending on the terms of the trust in which they are held. However, regardless of the terms of the trust, he is treated for CGT purposes as absolutely entitled to his shares as against the trustees. Thus the participant's CGT acquisition cost will equal the market value of the shares at the time of appropriation. And after appropriation the acts of the trustees are treated as acts of the participant, so that the eventual transfer of the shares to him will give rise to no CGT liability. [*FA 1978, s 53(5)*].

3.62 After the appropriation of the shares, the participant will be entitled to all dividends paid (see 3.28 above) and these will form part of his income for tax purposes. Where dividends are received from a company not resident in the UK, the trustees will be responsible for basic rate income tax (subject to any credit for overseas tax) and the participant will be liable for higher rate income tax only.

Disposal of shares

3.63 If the trustees dispose of any of the participant's shares before the release date, i.e. less than five years after appropriation, the participant is liable to income tax under Schedule E for the year of assessment in which the disposal takes place. (It will be recalled that the trustees are not permitted to dispose of shares except on the participant's instructions.) The one exception to the rule above is that a disposal of a participant's shares by his personal representatives after his death gives rise to no income tax liability. [*FA 1978, s 55(1)*].

3.64 Where shares have been appropriated to a participant at different times, disposals are matched with acquisitions on a 'first in, first out' (FIFO) basis for the purpose of the income tax calculations even if the participant instructs the trustees to sell specific shares. This rule minimises the income tax liability on a disposal (see 3.67 below). It has no application to the capital gains tax computations, which follow the normal rules. The profit sharing rules do not appear to cater for cases where shares of different classes have been appropriated to a participant at different times under the same scheme. However, the correct procedure must be to identify a disposal with an acquisition of shares of the same class on a FIFO basis. There can be no question of applying the FIFO basis so as to match a disposal of shares of one class with an appropriation of shares of another. [*FA 1978, s 55(6), 61(2)(3)(c)*].

Example 5

3.65 Shares have been appropriated to a participant in an approved profit sharing scheme as follows.

Date	No of shares	Initial market value (IMV)
		£
1.10.80	200	400
30.9.81	250	625
6.10.82	400	1,200

On 28.6.85 the participant directed the trustees to sell 250 shares. The shares sold will be identified with

200 shares appropriated on 1.10.80
50 shares appropriated on 30.9.81

3.66 The disposal of a participant's beneficial interest in his shares while the trustees remain the registered owners is simply treated as a disposal of the shares for the price obtained for the beneficial interest. However, when the beneficial interest vests in some person other than the participant by operation of law, e.g. in his trustee in bankruptcy, that is not treated as a disposal at all. [*FA 1978, s 55(7)*].

3.67 When a disposal occurs before the release date, the assessment is based on the 'appropriate percentage' of the 'locked-in value' of the relevant shares. [*FA 1978, s 55(1)*].

The 'appropriate percentage' depends on the time between the appropriation of the shares to the participant and their disposal, as follows.

Time from appropriation to disposal	Appropriate percentage
Under 4 years	100%
4 years or more but under 5	75%

[*FA 1978, s 54(7); FA 1980, s 46(5); FA 1985, s 45(3)*].

The 'locked-in value' is the 'initial market value' of the shares, i.e. the market value at the time of appropriation to the participant unless the Board and the trustees have agreed in writing to take the value at some earlier date. The locked-in value is treated as reduced by any 'capital receipts' (see 3.74 below) which have already given rise to income tax liability. If the proceeds of disposal are less than the locked-in value, income tax is payable on the appropriate percentage of the disposal proceeds only. [*FA 1978, s 55(2)(3)*].

It will be seen that the income tax liability is never based on a figure in excess of the initial market value of the shares. It is not based on the market value at the time of disposal. This may be contrasted with the rule for 'excess' and 'unauthorised' shares where the income tax charge is on the full value of the shares (see 3.89–3.98 below).

3.68 Where a participant loses his job on account of injury, disability or redundancy, or reaches pensionable age, before the fifth anniversary of the appropriation of shares to him, the appropriate percentage is 50%

and the higher percentages quoted in the table never apply. [*FA 1978, s 54(7)(c); FA 1980, s 46(5); FA 1985, s 45(3)*].

Example 6

3.69 The facts are the same as in Example 5. The proceeds of the sale on 28.6.85 are £525 (£2.10 per share). There were no capital receipts prior to sale.

In the case of the shares appropriated on 1.10.80, the locked-in value (£400) is less than the sale proceeds (£420). The income tax charge is therefore	
	£
£400 @ 75%	300
In the case of the shares appropriated on 30.9.81, the sale proceeds (£105) are less than the locked-in value (£125). The income tax charge is therefore:	
£105 @ 100% =	105
The total assessable under Schedule E for 1985/86 is therefore	£405

3.70 Market value must be substituted for the proceeds (if any) actually received on a disposal if

(*a*) the transfer is to the participant himself; or

(*b*) the Board consider that the disposal is not at arm's length and specifically direct that market value be used; or

(*c*) the disposal is of the participant's beneficial interest and takes place within the period of retention.

[*FA 1978, s 55(8)*].

3.71 The chargeable gain on a disposal is not reduced by any income tax assessment under these provisions. [*FA 1978, s 61(3)(a)*]. This is not unreasonable as the 'cost' figure in the capital gains tax computation would normally be the market value on appropriation, e.g. the 'initial market value'. As has been seen, it is only that initial value which is charged to income tax.

Payments made for rights

3.72 Where a participant has made one or more payments to the trustees to enable them to take up rights issues on his behalf, the payment(s) are deducted from the proceeds of sale to decide whether the proceeds exceed the locked-in value or vice versa. (No deduction is given where the cost of taking up a rights issue has been met out of the proceeds of sale of some of the rights.) Where only part of a holding is disposed of, only a proportion of the qualifying payment(s) can be deducted, namely the proportion which, immediately before the disposal, the market value of the shares disposed of bore to the market value of all the participant's shares held by the trustees. 'Shares' for this purpose includes securities allotted in a rights issue. [*FA 1978, s 55(4)(5)(9)*]. It is not possible to obtain double relief, and on any subsequent disposal only the balance of the payment(s), not deducted on the original disposal, can be taken into account. These rules seem to apply even if the shares disposed of were not actually involved in the rights issue. Suppose that a participant has shares of two classes appropriated to him, only one of which has been the subject of a rights issue. It seems that he will still be entitled to deduct a proportion of the cost of taking up the rights. Presumably this is unintentional.

Example 7

3.73 The facts are the same as in Examples 5 and 6.

On 1 October 1985 there is a rights issue of 1 for 5 at £1 each which the participant takes up. On 30 June 1986 he sells 360 shares at £2.60 per share. The share history before the disposal is as follows.

Date of appropriation	No of shares	Rights (1 for 5)	Total shares	Locked-in value (LIV)	Payment for rights
				£	£
30.9.81	200	40	240	500	40
6.10.82	400	80	480	1,200	80

The proceeds of sale will then be reduced as follows.

Date of appropriation	No of shares sold	Proceeds	Payment for rights	Net proceeds	Locked-in value (LIV)
		£	£	£	£
30.9.81	240	624	40	584	500
6.10.82	120	312	20	292	300

The income tax charge is therefore:	£
shares appropriated 30.9.81 £500 @ 75% =	375
" " 6.10.82 £292 @ 100% =	292
	£667

Capital receipts

3.74 Subject to 3.75 below, the term 'capital receipt' includes any money or money's worth received in respect of a participant's shares. [*FA 1978, s 56(1); FA 1982, s 42(1)*]. Examples of capital receipts are

(*a*) cash payments on reduction of share capital;

(*b*) cash payments made as part of a company reconstruction or amalgamation; and

(*c*) proceeds of sale of rights.

3.75 The following are specifically excluded from treatment as capital receipts

(*a*) payments treated as income for tax purposes apart from the profit sharing provisions, such as dividends;

(*b*) proceeds of disposal of shares, which are in any case taxable as income under the profit sharing provisions;

(*c*) new shares received in a company reconstruction or amalgamation; and

(*d*) proceeds of a sale of rights, if used to take up other rights.

[*FA 1978, s 56(2)(3)*].

3.76 If the participant or the trustees become entitled to a capital receipt before the release date (see 3.46 above), the participant is charged to income tax under Schedule E for the year of assessment in which entitlement arises. The charge is based on the appropriate percentage (see 3.67 above) of the capital receipt. From this must be deducted the 'appropriate allowance' for the year. The appropriate allowance is found by multiplying £20 by one plus the number of years in the five year period preceding the year in question in which shares were appropriated to the participant under the scheme, the maximum being £100. (Before 1986/87 substitute seven years for five and a maximum of £140 for £100). If the participant or trustees become entitled to more than one capital receipt in any one year, the appropriate allowance for that year will be set against the receipts in date order. [*FA 1978, s 56(1)(6); FA 1982, s 42(1)(2); FA 1985, s 45(4)*].

3.77 If the capital receipt exceeds the locked-in value of the shares (see 3.67 above), the income tax charge is based on the locked-in value, not the capital receipt. The calculation of the appropriate allowance is unaltered. [*FA 1978, s 56(4)*].

3.78 *Example 8*

1.4.82	1,000 shares at £1.05 each appropriated to participant.
7.4.86	Capital receipt of 5p per share (total £50).
31.10.86	Capital receipt of 20p per share (total £200).
27.2.87	The shares are sold for £2 each.

First capital receipt

	£
Capital receipt	50
Less: Appropriate allowance: £20 × (1 + 1)	40
Chargeable	£10

The appropriate percentage is 75%

	£	£	£
Therefore the income tax charge is £10 @ 75%		7	
Second capital receipt			
Capital receipt	200		
Less: Appropriate allowance	–		
	£200		
The appropriate percentage is 75%			
Therefore the income tax charge is £200 @ 75%		150	
		£157	157
Sale of shares			
LIV = initial market value		1,050	
Less: Capital receipts	50		
	200		
		250	
		£800	
The appropriate percentage is 75%			
Therefore the income tax charge is £800 @ 75%		£600	600
Sch E charge, 1986/87			£757

3.79 There is no income tax liability where entitlement to a capital receipt arises after a participant's death. [*FA 1978, s 56(5)*].

3.80 A capital receipt may count as a 'capital distribution' for capital gains tax purposes notwithstanding the income tax charge described in 3.76 above. [*FA 1978, s 61(3)(b)*]. Thus there may be a capital gains tax as well as an income tax liability. The capital gains tax liability is calculated in the normal way (see 3.99–3.104 below).

Company reconstructions

3.81 The profit sharing legislation provides special treatment for certain transactions in shares and securities in which a 'new holding' is equated with the 'original holding' for capital gains tax purposes, e.g.

(*a*) bonus issues;

(*b*) rights issues;

(*c*) alterations of the rights attaching to one of the classes of a company's share capital;

(*d*) conversion of securities into other securities or into shares;

(*e*) reductions of share capital;

(*f*) paper-for-paper takeovers; and

(*g*) schemes of reconstruction or amalgamation.

These are all referred to below as 'company reconstructions'. [*FA 1978, s 57(1)*].

3.82 Any shares or securities a participant receives in a company reconstruction (the 'new shares') are treated as identical with the shares in respect of which they were issued or which they otherwise represent (the 'corresponding shares'), and, with any corresponding shares retained by the participant, constitute a 'new holding'. However, the new holding will not include:

(*a*) redeemable shares or securities issued otherwise than wholly for new consideration; or

(*b*) bonus shares issued following a repayment of share capital; or

(*c*) shares issued as stock dividends.

[*FA 1978, s 57(2)–(4)*].

In all the above cases the issue of the shares will result in a charge to income tax under general tax law.

3.83 Subject to 3.87 below, a company reconstruction is not treated as involving any disposal of the original holding or acquisition of the new holding, but the new shares are treated as having been appropriated to the participant at the same time as the corresponding shares and as complying with the conditions listed in 3.36–3.42 above if those shares did so. [*FA 1978, s 57(4)*].

3.84 The initial market value (see 3.67 above) of the new holding is determined by ascertaining the locked-in value (see 3.67 above) of the original holding immediately before the reconstruction and apportioning this between the new shares and the corresponding shares on the basis of their respective market values immediately after the reconstruction. Obviously, if the corresponding shares have disappeared in the reconstruction the entire locked-in value will be attributed to the new shares. The locked-in value of the new holding will be its initial market value less any capital receipts after the reconstruction. [*FA 1978, s 57(5)*]. Capital receipts before the reconstruction will have been deducted in arriving at the initial market value of the new holding, as will any cash element in the reconstruction itself (see 3.87 below).

Example 9

3.85 Shares were appropriated to a participant as follows.

Date	No of shares	Initial market value (IMV)
		£
30.4.81	200	500
10.5.82	250	750

On 1 February 1984 there was a 1 for 2 bonus issue and on 31 May 1985 the participant sold 500 shares for £2,000.

The position immediately before the sale was as follows.

Date of appropriation	No of shares	Bonus shares	Total	Locked-in value (LIV) £
30.4.81	200	100	300	500
10.5.82	250	125	375	750

The shares sold will be identified as follows.

Date of appropriation	No of shares		Locked-in value (LIV) £
30.4.81	300		500
10.5.82	200 (out of 375)	$£750 \times \frac{200}{375}$	400

The income tax charge for 1985/86 will therefore be:

	£
£500 @ 75%	375
£400 @ 100%	400
	£775

3.86 *Example 10*

31 October 1980	500 shares in company A at £1 each appropriated.
1 November 1981	600 shares in company A at £1.50 each appropriated.
30 April 1983	Company A is taken over by company B and the shareholders receive one ordinary share and £1 15% debenture stock in company B for each share in company A.
30 June 1985	100 shares sold for £290, and £700 debenture stock sold for £770.

Before the takeover the 'original holding' comprises the following

(*a*) 500 shares in Company A with LIV £500

(*b*) 600 shares in company A with LIV £900

After the takeover the 'new shares' are as follows.

(*a*) For 500 'A': 500 'B' + £500 15% debentures with total LIV £500

(*b*) For 600 'A': 600 'B' + £600 15% debentures with total LIV £900

The total LIV of each holding must be apportioned between shares and debentures on the basis of their respective market values immediately after the takeover.

These were:

1 'B' share	£1.57½
£1 15% debenture	£1.05

The apportionment of the LIVs is therefore as follows.

(*a*) (i) 500 'B' shares £

$$£500 \times \frac{787.5}{787.5 + 525} = 300$$

(ii) £500 debentures

$$£500 \times \frac{525}{787.5 + 525} = 200$$

£500

(*b*) (i) 600 'B' shares

$$£900 \times \frac{945}{945 + 630} = 540$$

(ii) £600 debentures

$$£900 \times \frac{630}{945 + 630} = 360$$

£900

Using the identification rules (see 3.64 above) the disposals are identified as follows.

(*a*) 100 shares treated as appropriated 31 October 1980
£500 debentures treated as appropriated 31 October 1980

(*b*) £200 debentures treated as appropriated 1 November 1981

The LIVs of the holdings disposed of are therefore

	£
(*a*) 100 shares $£300 \times \frac{100}{500}$	60
£500 debentures	200
	£260
(*b*) £200 debentures $£360 \times \frac{200}{600}$	£120

It is clear that the LIVs are less than the proceeds of sale. The Schedule E charge for 1985/86 is therefore as follows.

	£
(*a*) £260 @ 75%	195
(*b*) £120 @ 100%	120
	£315

3.87 In some cases a company reconstruction involves the receipt of cash as well as shares and/or securities. This cash element constitutes a 'capital receipt' the treatment of which is described in 3.76–3.80 above. Entitlement is regarded as arising before the new holding comes into being and, for the purposes of 3.84 above, before the locked-in value of the original holding is ascertained. [*FA 1978, s 57(6)*]. Thus the cash element will reduce the initial market value of the new holding.

Example 11

3.88 Shares in A plc were appropriated to a participant as follows.

Date	No of shares	IMV
		£
30.6.81	100	500
1.7.82	150	900

On 30 September 1983 A plc was taken over by B plc. A plc's shareholders received 2 shares in B plc and 50p cash for each share in A plc. On 1 October 1985, 260 shares were sold for £2,600.

The capital receipt of 50p per share is treated as arising immediately before the takeover. The appropriate allowance (see 3.76 above) is

$$£20 \times (1 + 1 + 1) = £60.$$

The income tax charge for 1983/84 is therefore as follows.

Date of appropriation	No of shares	Capital receipt	Appropriate allowance	Net receipt	Appropriate percentage	Chargeable
		£	£	£		£
30.6.81	100	50	24	26	100%	26
1.7.82	150	75	36	39	100%	39
						£65

After the capital receipt the revised locked-in values are as follows.

Date of appropriation	No of shares	Original LIV	Capital receipt	Adjusted LIV
		£	£	£
30.6.81	100	500	50	450
1.7.82	150	900	75	825

After the takeover, the new holding of shares in B plc is as follows.

Date of appropriation	No of shares	IMV
		£
30.6.81	200	450
1.7.82	300	825

Using the rules in 3.64 above, the 260 shares sold on 1 October are identified as follows.

Shares appropriated	Total holding	Shares sold		LIV	Sale proceeds
				£	£
30.6.81	200	200		450	2,000
1.7.82	300	60	$£825 \times \frac{60}{300} =$	165	600

The income tax charge for 1985/86 is therefore

	£
£450 @ 75%	337
£165 @ 100%	165
	£502

Excess and unauthorised shares

3.89 Two of the conditions for the approval of a profit sharing scheme are that

(*a*) the scheme limits the value of the shares that can be appropriated to any one participant in any one year of assessment to 'the relevant amount' (see 3.33–3.35 above); and

(*b*) shares are not appropriated to individuals who are ineligible to participate.

Contravention of either of these conditions could lead to the withdrawal of approval from the scheme. However, a breach of these rules may take place quite innocently, and in that case the shares appropriated will simply be treated as 'excess' or 'unauthorised' shares. The scheme itself will not be affected.

3.90 If an individual is allocated shares in excess of the annual maximum (see 3.33–3.35 above) under one or more approved profit sharing schemes in which he is interested, the shares allocated to him after he has reached that maximum are 'excess shares'. If shares are appropriated to an individual under two or more schemes at the same time, the same proportion of the shares appropriated under each scheme is treated as exceeding the annual limit. [*FA 1978, s 58(1)(2); FA 1983, s 25(1)*].

3.91 'Unauthorised shares' are any shares—whether within the annual maximum or not—appropriated to an individual who is not eligible to participate in the scheme, by reason of the provisions discussed in 3.48–3.57 above. [*FA 1978, s 58(3)*].

3.92 Where there has been a company reconstruction (see 3.81 above) a 'new share' is treated as excess or unauthorised if the 'corresponding share' was excess or unauthorised. [*FA 1978, s 58(7)*].

Example 12

3.93 A participant's holding in an approved profit sharing scheme consists of 1,200 shares, 200 of which are 'excess'.

The company is taken over on the basis of £3 nominal 12% debentures for every 2 shares.

The participant is therefore entitled to £1,200 × $\frac{3}{2}$ = £1,800 nominal 12% debentures. Of these, £1,800 × $\frac{200}{1,200}$ = £300 count as 'excess'.

3.94 While the legislation draws a distinction between excess and unauthorised shares, there seems to be no difference between the treatment of the two categories of share for tax purposes.

3.95 The treatment of the appropriation of excess or unauthorised shares to a participant is exactly the same as that of the appropriation of any other shares under an approved profit sharing scheme. In other words, no Schedule E income tax liability arises. The major difference is that, in the case of excess or unauthorised shares, there is invariably an income tax charge at some later date.

3.96 A sale of shares (or any other occurrence that may give rise to a Schedule E assessment under the profit sharing provisions) is treated, as far as possible, as relating to shares which are not 'excess' or 'unauthorised' rather than to shares which are. But when there is a disposal of excess or unauthorised shares the 'locked-in value' (see 3.67 above) is their market value at the time of the disposal etc., not at the time of appropriation, and the 'appropriate percentage' is invariably 100% regardless of the period of ownership. Moreover 'excess' and 'unauthorised' shares which have not been disposed of by the release date (see 3.46 above), or by the death of the participant, are deemed to be disposed of at their market value at the earlier of those times. It will be appreciated, therefore, that the entire value of excess and unauthorised shares will inevitably be charged to income tax sooner or later. What is more, any attempt to sell them will be treated as far as possible as a sale of other shares.

Thus the income tax charge will be deferred until the maximum amount of capital growth has taken place. [*FA 1978, s 58(4)-(6)*].

3.97 *Example 13*

30.6.80 100 shares at £5 each appropriated to participant.
21.6.81 120 shares at £10 each appropriated to participant.
24.6.85 Sale of 110 shares at £15 each.
20 of the shares appropriated on 21.6.81 are 'excess' shares.

The shares sold will be identified with
(*a*) 100 shares appropriated on 30.6.80
(*b*) 10 'normal' shares appropriated on 21.6.81

	£	£
(*a*) Appropriate percentage 75% LIV	500	
Sale proceeds	1,500	
Income tax charge, 1985/86: £500 @ 75%		375
(*b*) Appropriate percentage 75% LIV	100	
Sale proceeds	150	
Income tax charge, 1985/86: £100 @ 75%		75
		£450

There is a deemed disposal of the 20 'excess' shares on the release date, 21.6.86, when the market value is £20 per share.

Appropriate percentage 100% LIV (market value)	£400	
Income tax charge, 1986/87: £400 @ 100%		£400

3.98 Where an individual disposes of his beneficial interest in shares during the period of retention (see 3.44 above) the shares concerned are treated as if they had been unauthorised shares. [*FA 1978, s 54(3)*]. That will not normally make any difference to the participant's income tax liability, as the appropriate percentage of such a receipt would be 100% anyway. But it will give rise to additional liability where the capital receipt exceeds the initial market value of the shares, because in the case of unauthorised shares the income tax charge is on the actual receipt not the initial market value. This may be contrasted with the rule for shares which are not excess or unauthorised, where the charge is on the lower of the initial market value and the capital receipt (see 3.67 above).

Capital gains tax

3.99 The application of the capital gains tax rules to approved profit sharing schemes has already been referred to, but the main points are summarised below.

3.100 For capital gains tax purposes, a participant is treated as absolutely entitled to his shares as against the trustees from the moment of appropriation. From that moment, the trustees are treated as bare trustees and any capital gains tax liability is the participant's (see 3.61 above). [*FA 1978, s 53(5)*].

3.101 The trustees are exempt from capital gains tax on appropriation of shares to a participant, provided that this occurs within eighteen months of the acquisition of the shares. To decide whether shares have been appropriated to participants within the eighteen month time limit, appropriations have to be matched with acquisitions on a 'first in, first out' (FIFO) basis. [*FA 1978, s 53(6)*].

3.102 Where the trustees do have a capital gains tax liability—for instance because they sell shares to meet administrative expenses—this is computed in the normal way, and the normal annual exemption for trustees applies. The capital gains tax treatment of the participants also follows the normal rules. The one point of difference is that, until the release date, the scheme shares will form a separate pool from any other shares of the same class held by the participant. [*CGTA 1979, s 65(5)*].

Example 14

3.103 Assume the facts are the same as in Examples 5, 6 and 7 (see 3.65, 3.69 and 3.73 above), namely

Date	Transaction	No of shares	Cost	Proceeds
			£	£
1.10.80	appropriation	200	400	
30.9.81	"	250	625	
6.10.82	"	400	1,200	
28.6.85	sale	250		525
1.10.85	rights issue	120	120	
30.6.86	sale	360		936

(*a*) The CGT position immediately before the disposal on 28.6.85 is as follows.

		£
'Frozen' pool		
200 shares appropriated	1.10.80	400
250 " "	30.9.81	625
450		£1,025
'New' pool		
400 shares appropriated	6.10.82	£1,200

(*b*) Sale on 28.6.85

For CGT purposes, the 250 shares sold on 28.6.85 will be matched with the 'new' pool acquired on 6.10.82 [*FA 1985, 19 Sch 19(2)*], and the allowable loss will be computed as shown in (*e*) below.

(*c*) Rights issue on 1.10.85

For CGT purposes, the rights issue will be allocated as follows.

	No of shares	Rights	Total	Original cost	Cost of rights	Total
				£	£	£
'Frozen' pool	450	90	540	1,025	90	1,115
'New' pool	150	30	180	450	30	480

(*d*) Sale on 30.6.86

For CGT purposes, the 360 shares sold on 30.6.86 will be matched with:

180 shares in the 'new' pool
180 „ „ „ 'frozen' pool
360

[*FA 1985, 19 Sch 19(2)(3)*]. The chargeable gain will be computed as shown in (*e*) below.

(*e*) *'New' pool*

Date	Event	RPI	Shares	Unindexed cost	Indexed pool
				£	£
6.10.82	Shares appropriated	324.5	400	1,200	
5.4.85	New pool created	373.9			
	$£1,200 \times \frac{373.9}{324.5}$				1,383
28.6.85	Sale of 250 shares	376.4			
	Indexation update				
	$£1,383 \times \frac{376.4 - 373.9}{373.9}$				9
			400	1,200	1,392
			(250)	(750)	(870)
			150	450	522
1.10.85	Rights issue	377.1			
	Indexation update				
	$£522 \times \frac{377.1 - 376.4}{376.4}$				1
					523
			30	30	30
			180	480	553
30.6.86	Sale of 180 shares	385.8			
	Indexation update				
	$£553 \times \frac{385.8 - 377.1}{377.1}$				13
			180	£480	£566

1985/86	Sale on 28.6.85		
	Allowable loss £525 – £870		(£345)
1986/87	Sale on 30.6.86		
	Allowable loss £468 – £566		(£98)

'Frozen' pool

	£	£
Sale proceeds, 30.6.86		468
Cost $£1{,}115 \times \frac{180}{540}$		372
		96
Indexation		
(i) Original cost		
$£1{,}025 \times \frac{180}{540} = £342$		
$£342 \times \frac{385.8 - 313.4}{313.4}$	79	
(ii) Rights		
$£90 \times \frac{180}{540} = £30$		
$£30 \times \frac{385.8 - 377.1}{377.1}$	1	
		80
Gain		16
Loss on 'new pool'		(98)
Allowable loss		(£82)

If the market value of the shares at 31 March 1982 was more than £2.28 a share (£1,025 ÷ 450), the indexation relief on the 'frozen' pool could be based on that value (instead of original cost), provided that an election is made by 5 April 1989. If the 31 March 1982 market value were £3, for example, the indexation relief at (i) above would be

$$150 \times £3 \times \frac{385.8 - 313.4}{313.4} = £104, \text{ instead of } £80.$$

Example 15

3.104 Assume the facts are the same as in Example 8 (see 3.78 above), namely that 1,000 shares worth £1.05 each were appropriated to the participant on 1.4.82.

On 7.4.86 there is a capital receipt of 5p per share (total £50). Assume that at that time the value of the shares was £1.30 each. The receipt is 'small' compared with the value of the shares and may therefore be deducted from the original cost of £1,050.

	£
Cost	1,050
Less: Capital receipt	50
	£1,000

On 31.10.86 there is a capital receipt of 20p per share (total £200). Assume that at that time the value of the shares was £1.40 each. The receipt is not 'small', so the gain or loss must be calculated.

	£	£
Capital receipt		200
Cost £1,000 × $\frac{200}{1,600}$		125
Unindexed gain		75
Indexation		
(i) on original cost		
£1,050 × $\frac{200}{1,600}$ = £131		
RPI for October 1986, say 395.0		
RPI for April 1982, 319.7		
£131 × $\frac{395.0 - 319.7}{319.7}$	31	
(ii) on capital receipt		
£50 × $\frac{200}{1,600}$ = £6		
RPI for October 1986, say 395.0		
RPI for April 1986, 385.3		
£6 × $\frac{395.0 - 385.3}{385.3}$	(1)	
		30
Chargeable gain		£45

On 27.2.87 the shares are sold for £2 each.

		£
Sale proceeds		2,000
Cost (£1,000 − £125)		875
Unindexed gain		c/f 1,125
Indexation		
(i) on original cost		
£1,050 − £131 = £919		
RPI for February 1987, say 399.7		
RPI for April 1982, 319.7		
£919 × $\frac{399.7 - 319.7}{319.7}$	c/f 230	

	£	£
	b/f 230	b/f 1,125
(ii) on capital receipt £50 − £6 = £44		
RPI for February 1987, say 399.7		
RPI for April 1986, 385.3		
$£44 \times \frac{399.7 - 385.3}{385.3}$	(2)	
	—	228
Chargeable gain		£897

The Schedule E charge

3.105 Any Schedule E charge in respect of a participant's shares falls in the year of assessment in which the relevant capital receipt arises or the relevant disposal is made. However, the income assessed is not included in the participant's emoluments and therefore is not eligible for, say, the 100% deduction for long absences abroad provided by *FA 1977, 7 Sch 1*. Amounts assessable under the profit sharing provisions are treated as ordinary Schedule E income for the purposes of the PAYE regulations. [*FA 1978, s 59(5)*].

The application of PAYE

3.106 On receiving a capital receipt or the proceeds of sale of shares, the trustees are required to pay to the company the amount, if any, on which Schedule E income tax is chargeable. In the case of a capital receipt, this will be the appropriate percentage of the capital receipt or, if lower, of the locked-in value of the shares. In the case of a disposal, it will be the appropriate percentage of the locked-in value of the shares or, if lower, of the proceeds of disposal. The company must then deduct income tax under PAYE (as if the amount in question constituted emoluments) before passing the balance on to the participant. [*FA 1978, s 59(1)*]. The non-taxable part of the sum received by the trustees is paid by them direct to the participant.

3.107 In the case of a group scheme, the payment must be made to the participating company of which the participant is a director or employee at the time. If there is more than one such company, the Board may direct which of them is to receive the payment and account for PAYE. If there is no such company, or if the Board do not consider it practicable for any such company to account for PAYE, they may direct that the trustees be responsible for PAYE themselves. Alternatively, they may nominate another company for this task so long as the trustees and all the companies concerned agree. [*FA 1978, s 59(2)–(4)*].

3.108 When PAYE is operated by the trustees or by a company of which the participant is not a director or employee, the income tax deduction is at the basic rate only. [*SI 1973 No 334, reg 16*]. This is because the legislation requires PAYE to be operated as if the participant were a former employee of the trustees or of the company. [*FA 1978, s 59(3)(4)*].

3.109 Where, before the release date, the trustees transfer shares to the participant, the payment he is obliged to make to them (see 3.46 above) is treated as a PAYE deduction on account of the income tax liability resulting from the transfer. [*FA 1978, s 59(6)*].

3.110 Money arising from excess or unauthorised shares (see 3.89–3.98 above) is treated in exactly the same way as that arising from any other scheme shares. This is perhaps surprising, as the Schedule E charge is not restricted to the market value of such shares at the time of appropriation. But, unless the Board direct otherwise, PAYE is to be operated as if such shares were not excess or unauthorised shares. [*FA 1978, s 59(7)*].

Payments to the trustees

3.111 A payment to the trustees to enable them to acquire scheme shares will be allowed as a trading expense or as a management expense if, and only if, it is made by a company which has established a profit sharing scheme (or, in the case of a group scheme, by any participating company) and

(*a*) the trustees use the money in acquiring scheme shares before the end of the 'relevant period'; or

(*b*) the money is required to meet the reasonable expenses of the trustees in administering the scheme.

It is considered that (*a*) above is wide enough to cover incidental costs of acquiring the shares as well as the actual share price. [*FA 1978, s 60(1)(2)*].

3.112 The 'relevant period' is the nine months following the end of the period of account in which the payment is charged as an expense. However, the Revenue have discretion to extend this period if they see fit. In applying the time limit, one has to assume that the trustees use money paid to them on a 'first in, first out' (FIFO) basis. In the case of a group scheme, a payment by a participating company will not be deductible unless it is used in acquiring shares which are appropriated to that company's directors and employees. It will therefore be advisable to identify and segregate the contributions made by each participating company. [*FA 1978, s 60(2)–(4)*].

3.113 The trustees may purchase shares from existing shareholders (including participants in the scheme) or they may subscribe for new shares to be issued by the company. If they subscribe for new shares, there will be no reduction in the company's working capital; the funds paid out to the trustees will simply be repaid in the form of share capital.

In fact, the working capital will be increased by the tax savings which the payments attract.

Example 16

3.114 Two companies pay corporation tax at the small companies rate (30%). One makes a payment of £10,000 to the trustees of an approved profit sharing scheme. Assuming that the money is used to subscribe for new shares, the respective cash flow positions of the two companies will be as follows.

	Company A		*Company B*	
		Cash outflow		*Cash outflow*
	£000	*£000*	*£000*	*£000*
Trading profit	100		100	
Less: Payment to trustees			10	10
Taxable profit	100		90	
Corporation tax at 30%	30	30	27	27
	70		63	
Share issue				(10)
Net outflow of cash		30		27

3.115 There is no statutory limit on the amount a company may set aside for the purposes of a profit sharing scheme. However, if a company has institutional investors the investment committee guidelines (see Chapter 7) may well be relevant and are likely to prove the limiting factor. There is no need for a company to allocate a fixed sum of money or a fixed percentage of profit to the scheme each year. Indeed, it would be permissible to use an approved profit sharing scheme to enable directors and employees to share the rewards of a single, exceptionally successful, year's trading. If a company were to bind itself legally to make yearly contributions of a fixed amount these might well constitute annual payments which would have to be made under deduction of basic rate income tax [*ICTA 1970, s 53*] and would be subject to additional rate income tax in the hands of the trustees. [*FA 1973, s 16*]. Such a commitment is unnecessary and is better avoided.

The position of the trustees

3.116 The provisions refer to the trustees acquiring shares, not necessarily subscribing for shares. Thus, as has been seen, they may either purchase existing shares or subscribe for new shares. Generally speaking, the company will find it more attractive if they subscribe for new shares (see 3.113 above). But where there is no scope for the issue of additional shares, the trustees' ability to purchase existing shares may well prove useful. To take one instance, the investment committee guidelines restrict the percentage of a company's share capital that can be subscribed for (as opposed to purchased) by the trustees of an approved profit sharing scheme. Where this restriction would otherwise prevent the trustees from acquiring more shares, the purchase of existing shares may prove to be the solution.

3.117 There will often be some delay between the acquisition of shares by the trustees and the appropriation of those shares to the participants. In the interim, dividends may be received and the shares may increase in value. However, provided that the trustees appropriate the shares to participants within 18 months of acquisition, the dividends will not attract the additional rate income tax normally payable by the trustees of discretionary settlements and no capital gains tax liability will arise on the appropriation itself. The tax credits attaching to dividends simply serve to discharge the trustees' liability to basic rate income tax. To decide whether shares have been appropriated to participants within the 18 month time limit, appropriations have to be linked with acquisitions on a 'first in, first out' (FIFO) basis. [*FA 1978, s 53(6)*]. Shares which have not been appropriated to a participant may be sold by the trustees, for instance to meet expenses, but capital gains tax will be payable on any gain that arises, subject to the normal annual exemption available to trustees.

3.118 Where before the release date a participant sells the beneficial interest in his shares to the trustees (see 3.46 above), the trustees must treat the price payable to him as proceeds received from a third party, i.e. they must deduct income tax under PAYE before making payment to the participant. [*FA 1978, s 59(1A); FA 1980, s 46(8)*].

3.119 For inheritance tax purposes, an approved profit sharing scheme counts as a privileged trust for the benefit of employees. It is therefore exempt from the inheritance tax charges which normally fall upon discretionary trusts (the ten year charge and the exit charge). Furthermore, if an employee acquires an interest in possession in part of the trust fund (e.g. on the appropriation of shares to him) that interest is ignored. No inheritance tax charge arises on its creation or on its termination. [*IHTA 1984, s 86*].

3.120 The trustees will be responsible for completing tax returns and paying basic rate and, where appropriate, higher rate income tax and capital gains tax in the same way as the trustees of any other discretionary trust.

Provision of information

3.121 The Board may require any person to supply such information as they consider necessary for the purposes of the profit sharing provisions. In particular, they may call for information

(*a*) to determine whether to approve a scheme, or to withdraw an approval previously given; and (*b*) to determine the tax liability of any participant in a scheme.

Such information must be required by a written notice, and the recipient must be given not less than thirty days to reply. [*FA 1978, s 53(7)*].

Returns

3.122 The trustees are required to submit annual returns to Technical Division (Employee Share Schemes) giving details of appropriation of shares, capital receipts and company reconstructions as indicated below.

3.123 For each appropriation in a particular year of assessment the trustees will be required to show on the return

(*a*) the date of appropriation;

(*b*) a description of the shares;

(*c*) the total number of shares appropriated;

(*d*) the market value of each share at that time;

(*e*) the number of participants; and

(*f*) the largest appropriation to any one participant.

3.124 The information required in respect of each capital receipt will include

(*a*) the date of entitlement;

(*b*) the value of the receipt per share; and

(*c*) the revised locked-in value of each appropriation affected.

In the case of a company reconstruction the trustees will be required to state

(*a*) the nature and effect of the reconstruction; and

(*b*) the revised locked-in value for each class of share involved.

Penalties

3.125 There are the normal penalties for failure to provide information required by a notice under 3.121 above. [*TMA 1970, s 98; FA 1978, s 53(8)*].

Chapter 4

Savings-related Share Option Schemes

Outline

4.1 In outline, savings-related share option schemes work as follows. The employer company grants directors and employees options to subscribe for new ordinary shares. The option holders then make regular savings under a SAYE contract. When the SAYE contract matures at the end of five, or in some cases seven, years, the option may be exercised. Thereupon, the accumulated savings are injected back into the company in the form of additional share capital.

4.2 One of the main attractions of an approved savings-related share option scheme is that it offers directors and employees exemption from the income tax liability that may otherwise arise where share options are granted or exercised.

4.3 Like approved profit sharing schemes, savings-related share option schemes are not selective. They must be open to every full-time director and employee who has completed a qualifying period of service. This qualifying period must not exceed five years. And all the participants must benefit from the scheme on similar terms, subject to variations depending on length of service, level of remuneration or similar factors.

4.4 Unlike approved profit sharing schemes, savings-related share option schemes are funded by the participants, whose savings are made out of taxed income.

4.5 The value of the shares that can be acquired under a savings-related share option scheme is restricted by the terms of the SAYE contract. At present the maximum that can be saved each month is £100. Thus the schemes provide for employee share-holding on a comparatively modest scale.

4.6 In general, the price to be paid on exercise of an option must not be less than 90% of the market value of the shares when the option was granted.

4.7 Once the director or employee has exercised the option he is as free to do what he likes with his shares as any other shareholder of the same class and if he sells them he will only be liable to capital gains tax.

4.8 For the employee, a savings-related share option scheme can be seen as a useful means of regular saving with the added attraction of an income tax free profit on the shares if the company is successful. For the employer, there is the further consideration that the proceeds of the SAYE contracts will be injected back into the company in the form of additional share capital.

Who may establish a scheme

4.9 Any body corporate may establish a savings-related share option scheme and obtain approval under these provisions. [*FA 1980, 10 Sch 1(1)*]. The body establishing the scheme need not be incorporated or resident in the UK. And, if it is incorporated in the UK, it need not be a company formed under the Companies Acts. It may, for instance, be a chartered company. However, it must be in a position to establish a scheme complying with the rules described in this chapter. It must be able, inter alia, to grant its directors and employees options over shares satisfying the conditions described in 4.21 to 4.53 below. And, unless at least some of the individuals participating in the scheme are within the UK tax net, there will be little point in going to the trouble of obtaining Revenue approval.

Scope of schemes

4.10 In many cases, the benefits of a savings-related share option scheme will be restricted to the directors and employees of the company which has established it. But where the company running such a scheme is the parent company of a group, the scheme may extend to the directors and employees of any of its subsidiaries. A scheme for a parent company and its subsidiaries is known as a 'group scheme', and any company which is included in the scheme (there is no need to include every company in the group) is referred to as a 'participating company'. For this purpose, a subsidiary is any company over which the parent has control. 'Control' has the meaning given in *ICTA 1970, s 534*. [*FA 1980, 10 Sch 1(3), 26(1)*].

4.11 It is possible that a parent company which is in turn under the control of another company could establish a group scheme to extend to the directors and employees of its subsidiaries. But this scheme could not extend to the directors and employees of its holding company. This subject is discussed in 3.16 above, where there is an example illustrating a group scheme.

Approval procedure

4.12 A company which has established a savings-related share option scheme may apply to the Board for approval. The application must be in writing and must contain such information and be supported by such evidence as the Board may require. [*FA 1980, 10 Sch 1(1)(2)*]. There is no special form of application, but the following information should be provided.

(*a*) The name and registered office of the company which has established the scheme, the tax district to which it makes its returns and its reference number in that district. This information is also required for the company whose shares are to be subject to the options, if that is not the company which has established the scheme, and, in the case of a 'group scheme' (see 4.10 above), for all the companies to which the scheme extends.

(*b*) The memorandum and articles of association of the company whose shares are to be used, and any relevant amendments.

(*c*) The rules of the scheme.

(*d*) The form of contract under which the option is to be granted.

(*e*) A declaration by the company which has established the scheme that the shares to be used will satisfy the conditions in 4.37–4.41 below.

(*f*) If the shares which are to be subject to the options are not shares in the company which has established the scheme or are shares in a company which is under the control of another company, a further declaration indicating precisely how the conditions in 4.38 below are met.

(*g*) Any other documents which will be issued to participants and/or shareholders in connection with the scheme.

4.13 Applications for approval should be addressed to: Inland Revenue, Technical Division (Employee Share Schemes), Somerset House, London WC2R 1LB.

4.14 The legislation envisages that approval will be obtained only after a scheme has been drawn up and adopted by a company. There is no provision for the company to obtain advance confirmation that the terms of a scheme which it proposes to establish will qualify. A common procedure is to adopt a scheme and then amend the rules if need be in order to obtain approval. In addition, it is understood that the Technical Division (Employee Share Schemes) is prepared to comment informally on draft documentation and to discuss particular points of difficulty in advance of a formal application for approval.

4.15 The Board do not have any discretion with regard to the approval of savings-related share option schemes. They are obliged to approve a scheme provided that it meets the requirements listed at 4.20 below and does not include 'features . . . which are neither essential nor reasonably incidental' to its purpose of providing shares for directors and employees. [*FA 1980, 10 Sch 1(1); FA 1984, s 39(2)*]. A provision allowing the payment of cash in lieu of shares would violate this condition.

4.16 If a scheme was conditionally approved before 25 July 1986 without evidence that the exercise price satisfied the requirement in 4.23 below, the approval will be ineffective if the price is later found not to do so. [*FA 1980, 10 Sch 2; FA 1986, s 25(2)*].

4.17 Any alteration to an approved scheme, however minor, must itself be approved by the Board, or the scheme as a whole will automatically lose its approved status from the date the alteration is made. [*FA 1980, 10 Sch 3(2)*]. This is an important point which can all too easily be overlooked in practice. It is therefore advisable to include in the rules of the scheme a provision that no alteration is to be made without the Board's prior approval.

4.18 Even where there is no alteration to a scheme the Board's approval may be withdrawn if

(*a*) the Board ceases to be satisfied that the conditions listed in 4.20 below are met; or

(*b*) the company fails to provide any information requested by the Board under the provisions discussed in 4.63 below.

However, where a director or employee has obtained an option prior to the withdrawal of approval he can exercise that option after the withdrawal and still enjoy the tax privileges which would have been available had the approval not been withdrawn. [*FA 1980, 10 Sch 3(1); FA 1984, s 39(4)*].

4.19 Where the Board

(*a*) refuses to approve a scheme; or

(*b*) refuses to confirm a conditional approval (see 4.16 above); or

(*c*) refuses to approve an alteration; or

(*d*) withdraws an approval previously given,

the company may appeal to the Special Commissioners within 30 days of notification. [*FA 1980, 10 Sch 4*]. It should be noted that the participants, who may be most seriously affected by the Board's decision, do not have any right of appeal.

Conditions for approval

4.20 If it is to obtain approval a scheme must satisfy a number of conditions. These are discussed below under the following main headings

(*a*) general conditions (see 4.21 below);

(*b*) monetary limits (see 4.22 below);

(*c*) the option price (see 4.23–4.24 below);

(*d*) the dates when options may be exercised (see 4.25–4.36 below);

(*e*) conditions relating to the scheme shares (see 4.37–4.41 below);

(*f*) conditions relating to the participants (see 4.42–4.52 below); and

(*g*) conditions relating to the transfer of options (see 4.53 below).

General

4.21 The scheme must provide for directors and employees ('the participants') to obtain options to acquire shares which comply with the conditions described in 4.37–4.41 below ('the scheme shares'). The scheme shares must be paid for out of repayments, including interest and bonus, made under a special SAYE series linked to the savings-related share option scheme and approved by the Board for the purpose. The rules of the scheme must require that, so far as possible, a participant's SAYE contributions will secure him a repayment equivalent to the price of the shares he is entitled to acquire. [*FA 1980, 10 Sch 5, 13(1)*].

Monetary limits

4.22 It is a condition of approval of a scheme that an employee's SAYE contributions must not exceed £100 per month. This limit includes contributions to any linked SAYE scheme. Moreover the scheme must not impose a minimum contribution exceeding £10 per month. The Treasury may amend the £100 and £10 limits by way of statutory instrument. [*FA 1980, 10 Sch 13(2)(3); FA 1984, s 39(5)*].

Option price

4.23 The price at which an option obtained under a savings-related share option scheme may be exercised must be stated at the time when that option is granted. It must not be manifestly less than 90% of the market value of shares of that class at that time, or at such earlier time (not normally more than 30 days before the grant of the option) as the Board and the company agree in writing. However, provision may be made to vary the stated price to take account of any alterations in the company's share capital, e.g. bonus issues or rights issues. [*FA 1980, 10 Sch 14*]. It will be appreciated that these provisions merely lay down a minimum price at which options may be exercised under an approved scheme. There is no objection to setting the price higher and indeed in many cases this may be considered appropriate.

4.24 Where the shares are quoted, the market value at the time of the grant of the option will be easy to ascertain. Where the shares are not quoted, the market value will have to be agreed with the Inland Revenue's Share Valuation Division.

Date of exercise of option

4.25 With the exceptions discussed in 4.28–4.35 below, options must not be exercisable before the 'bonus date'. The 'bonus date' is the date on which the SAYE repayments fall due, assuming no delayed contributions. In practice, this means that options will usually be exercisable either after five years (to coincide with the five-year bonus under the SAYE contract) or after seven years (to coincide with the seven-year bonus). Which category an option falls into must be determined at the time of grant. In the case of a seven-year option, the maximum bonus must be taken into account. Since SAYE contracts provide for the repayment date to be postponed for one month for each delayed contribution (up to a maximum of six, when the SAYE contract lapses), the first exercise date may in practice fall anywhere between five years and five years six months (in the case of a five-year option) or between seven years and seven years six months (in the case of a seven-year option) after grant. [*FA 1980, 10 Sch 6*].

Example 1

4.26 Suppose that a participant wishes to save £45 a month. At the time when he is granted an option the scheme shares are worth £1 each and the exercise price is 90p a share. The alternatives are as follows.

(*a*) If he is granted a five-year option and no bonus is taken into account he will get an option over 3,000 shares ($45 \times 60 \times \frac{100}{90}$).

(*b*) If he is granted a five-year option and the bonus is taken into account he will get an option over 3,700 shares (3,000 as above plus five-year bonus $45 \times 14 \times \frac{100}{90}$).

(*c*) If he is granted a seven-year option he will have an option over 4,400 shares (3,000 as above plus seven-year bonus $45 \times 28 \times \frac{100}{90}$).

It should be noted, however, that the rules of a particular scheme may restrict the alternatives which can be chosen.

4.27 With the exception noted in 4.28 below, options must not be exercisable more than six months after the bonus date. [*FA 1980, 10 Sch 11*].

4.28 The scheme must provide that if a participant dies before the bonus date (see 4.25 above), any options he holds may be exercised up to, but not more than, twelve months after his death and that, if he dies in the six months after the bonus date, any such options may be exercised up to twelve months after the bonus date. [*FA 1980, 10 Sch 7*].

4.29 It is not normally permissible to exercise an option after resigning from one's employment. But a scheme must contain rules providing for the exercise of options

(*a*) after resignation, and

(*b*) before the normal exercise date,

in certain prescribed circumstances.

4.30 Thus the scheme must permit the exercise of options within six months of the holder's reaching state pensionable age (65 for men, 60 for women), whether or not he remains in employment thereafter. [*FA 1980, 10 Sch 8, 9*].

4.31 If a participant resigns as a result of injury, disability or redundancy, or of reaching contractual retirement age, the scheme must permit him to exercise any options he holds up to six months after his resignation. [*FA 1980, 10 Sch 8*].

4.32 If for any other reason he ceases to hold the employment under which he is eligible to participate, the scheme must, subject to 4.34(*e*) below, require him to forfeit any options acquired in the previous three years. If he holds options which were acquired more than three years previously, the scheme may either require him to forfeit them or permit him to exercise them within six months of resignation. [*FA 1980, 10 Sch 8; FA 1986, s 25(3)*]. The rules of the scheme may prescribe circumstances in which such options may or may not be exercised, but they cannot give the company a discretion in individual cases.

Example 2

4.33 John Smith, a participant in a savings-related share option scheme run by A plc, was born on 1 July 1920. He was granted a five-year option on 1 July 1983. No retirement age is specified in his contract of employment, but he in fact retires on 30 June 1987.

John Smith may exercise his option

(*a*) from 1 July to 31 December 1985, i.e. within six months of reaching state pension age; or

(*b*) if and only if the rules of the A plc scheme permit, from 1 July to 31 December 1987, i.e. within six months of retirement.

Thus if Smith fails to exercise his option by 31 December 1985 and the rules of the scheme do not permit him to exercise the option after retirement, it will lapse. If Smith had remained in employment another year, he would have been entitled to exercise the option at the normal date.

4.34 Events affecting the company whose shares are scheme shares could make it desirable for participants to be able to exercise their options early. Accordingly the scheme may (but need not) permit the exercise of options

(*a*) where there has been a change of control of the company as a result of a general offer for all the shares or for all the shares of the same class as the scheme shares;

(*b*) where the Court has sanctioned a compromise or arrangement in connection with a scheme of reconstruction or amalgamation of the company under *CA 1985, s 425*;

(*c*) where any person has become bound or entitled to acquire the shares of a dissenting minority in the company under *CA 1985, ss 428–430*;

(*d*) where the company has passed a resolution for voluntary winding up; and

(*e*) where a participant ceases to hold an employment which makes him eligible to benefit under the scheme because

  (i) his employer company ceases to be under the control of the company running the scheme; or

  (ii) the business with which his job is concerned is transferred to a company under different control.

In the case of (*a*), (*b*), (*d*) and (*e*) above, the scheme must not permit the exercise of options more than six months after the relevant event. In the case of (*c*), the scheme may permit the exercise of options so long as the person concerned remains bound or entitled to buy out the minority. [*FA 1980, 10 Sch 10(1); Companies Consolidation (Consequential Provisions) Act 1985, 2 Sch; FA 1986, s 25(4)*].

If a scheme approved before 1 August 1986 is altered before 1 August 1988 to include a provision of the kind described in (*e*) above, the company is free to apply the provision to options obtained before the alteration takes effect even where the relevant employment has already ceased, provided that the date of cessation was after 17 March 1986. In such cases a participant may be able to exercise an option after his employment with the company has ceased, despite the fact that, but for the new provision, he would have been ineligible to do so. The application of the provision is not itself treated as a right to acquire shares under the scheme. The alteration will need the Board's approval in the normal way. [*FA 1986, s 25(8)(9)*].

4.35 For the purposes of 4.31, 4.32 and 4.34 above, a person is not to be treated as having resigned unless he no longer holds any office or employment with the company running the scheme, with any company which that company controls, or with any associated company. [*FA 1980, 10 Sch 12; FA 1986, s 25(5)*]. 'Associated company' has the meaning given in *ICTA 1970, s 302*, except that a company no longer under common control does not count as an associated company merely because it was under common control at some time in the preceding year. [*FA 1980, 10 Sch 26(1); FA 1982, s 40(8)*].

4.36 Since an option can only be exercised to the extent that the shares can be paid for with SAYE repayments (see 4.21 above), an early exercise of an option as permitted by 4.28–4.35 above will inevitably be a partial exercise of an option. The unexercised part of the option will lapse.

The shares

4.37 The scheme shares must form part of the ordinary share capital of

(*a*) the company which established the scheme; or

(*b*) a company having control of the company which established the scheme; or

(*c*) a company which is a member of a consortium owning either the company in (*a*) or the company in (*b*) and which itself owns beneficially not less than 15% of the consortium company in question; or

(*d*) a company which has control of the consortium member in (*c*).

[*FA 1980, 10 Sch 15*].

'Control' has the meaning given in *ICTA 1970, s 534*. A company is a member of a consortium owning another company if it is one of a number of companies owning between them not less than 75% of the other company's ordinary share capital and each owning not less than 5% of that ordinary share capital. [*FA 1980, 10 Sch 26(1)(5); FA 1986, s 23(5)*]. 'Ordinary share capital' has the meaning given in *ICTA 1970, s 526(5)*, and therefore includes participating preference shares.

4.38 The scheme shares must be

(*a*) quoted shares; or

(*b*) unquoted shares in a company which is not under the control of any other company; or

(*c*) unquoted shares in a company which is under the control of a quoted company (other than a quoted company which is, or would if resident in the UK be, a close company).

'Control' has the meaning given in *ICTA 1970, s 534*. [*FA 1980, 10 Sch 16, 26(1)*].

Thus a scheme for, say, directors and employees of a trading subsidiary in an unquoted group is likely to rely on the shares of the parent company. The shares of the trading subsidiary cannot be scheme shares. It is apparently considered that the profits of a subsidiary can too easily be manipulated to the benefit or detriment of employee shareholders.

4.39 The shares must be fully paid up, must not be redeemable, and must not be subject to any restrictions not attaching to all shares of the same class, with the following exception.

It is permissible for the company's articles of association to require that all shares held by directors and employees be sold on cessation of employment; and, where a share option is exercised after employment has ceased, the articles may require that the shares be sold immediately after acquisition. However, the articles must require that the shares be sold for cash, and must prescribe the terms of sale. What is more, these terms must apply to all holders of shares of the same class, not just to directors and employees. In other words, the terms of sale must form part of general disposal provisions. [*FA 1980, 10 Sch 17; FA 1986, s 22(2)(4)*].

4.40 For this purpose, the term 'restriction' includes any contract, agreement, arrangement, or condition which

(*a*) limits a person's freedom to dispose of his shares, of any interest in them or of the proceeds of their sale; or

(*b*) limits his freedom to exercise any right conferred by those shares; or

(*c*) might make such a disposal or exercise disadvantageous to him or to any person connected with him. [*FA 1980, 10 Sch 18*].

'Connected person' here has the meaning given in *ICTA 1970, s 533*.

However, restrictions similar to those in the Stock Exchange 'Model Code for Securities Transactions by Directors of Listed Companies' issued in November 1984 will be ignored. [*FA 1982, s 41; FA 1986, s 23(4)*].

4.41 If the company has more than one class of ordinary share capital, the majority of the shares of the class to which the scheme shares belong must *either* be 'employee-control shares' *or* be held by persons other than

(*a*) persons who acquired their shares in pursuance of a right conferred on them or an opportunity afforded to them as directors or employees; or

(*b*) trustees for such shareholders (e.g. the trustees of an approved profit sharing scheme); or

(*c*) in the case of unquoted shares, any company which controls the company whose shares are scheme shares or of which that company is an associated company (as defined in *ICTA 1970, s 302*).

'Employee-control shares' are shares held by present or former directors or employees of the company or of a company it controls who together are able, as holders of those shares, to control the company in question.

[*FA 1980, 10 Sch 19; FA 1986, s 23(1)–(3)*].

The participants

4.42 The conditions relating to the participants have the effect of dividing a company's directors and employees into three categories (*a*) those who must be eligible to participate under the rules of any approved scheme (see 4.43–4.47 below);

(*b*) those who must be excluded from benefit by the rules of any approved scheme (see 4.48–4.51 below); and

(*c*) those whose inclusion or exclusion is optional and may vary from scheme to scheme (see 4.52 below).

4.43 With the exceptions noted in 4.48–4.51 below, the scheme must be open on similar terms to every full-time director or employee of the company—and in the case of a group scheme, of any participating company—whose earnings are taxable under Schedule E, Case I and who has completed a qualifying period of service (which may not exceed five years). [*FA 1980, 10 Sch 20(1)*].

4.44 There is no definition of the term 'full-time director or employee', but it is understood that the Revenue regard a director or employee as 'full-time' if he spends at least 25 hours a week working for his company.

4.45 There are provisions designed to counter attempts to restrict the benefit of savings-related share option schemes to chosen personnel. Thus not only must the scheme be open on similar terms to all directors and employees who satisfy the criteria in 4.43 above, but all those who decide to participate, even if they do not satisfy those criteria but are eligible to participate under the rules of a particular scheme (see 4.52 below), must in fact do so on similar terms. This does not mean on identical terms, and the fact that the number of shares under option to participants depends on salary level, length of service and similar factors will not be taken to imply that they do not all participate on similar terms. On the other hand, arbitrary discrimination is not permissible. [*FA 1980, 10 Sch 20; FA 1984, s 39(6)*].

4.46 It is not clear what other factors may be taken into account in determining the level of an individual's participation in addition to salary and length of service. However, the profitability of the company for which he works would clearly merit consideration.

4.47 The Board must also be satisfied that the scheme does not discourage any employees or former employees from participating if they fulfil the requirements in 4.43 above. And, where the company is a member of a group, the scheme must not concentrate its benefits wholly or mainly on the directors or highest paid employees of companies in the group. This rule is intended to prevent the use of a single company to employ all the group's directors and senior executives with the object of establishing a savings-related share option scheme for their benefit alone. For this purpose, a group comprises a parent company and any companies over which it has control. [*FA 1980, 10 Sch 1(1)(aa)(ab)(1A); FA 1984, s 39(2)(3)*]. 'Control' has the meaning given in *ICTA 1970, s 534*. [*FA 1980, 10 Sch 26(1)*]. There is an example of the kind of arrangement this provision is aimed at in 3.52 above.

4.48 The rules of the scheme must provide that nobody other than a director or employee of the company, or of a participating company in the case of a group scheme, is eligible to have options granted to him under the scheme. However, there are certain cases where a participant may exercise an option after he has ceased to be a director or employee (see 4.28–4.35 above). [*FA 1980, 10 Sch 21; FA 1986, s 24(6)*].

4.49 There is now no restriction on a director or employee being granted options under more than one savings-related share option scheme in any one year of assessment, provided that the monetary limits are not exceeded (see 4.22 above).

4.50 An individual must not be eligible to benefit under a scheme if he has, or in the preceding twelve months has had, a 'material interest' in a close company which is

(*a*) the company whose shares are to be scheme shares; or

(*b*) a company controlling that company or a member of a consortium owning that company.

[*FA 1980, 10 Sch 23(1)*].

In determining whether a person has a material interest in a company, the interests of his associates must be taken into account. 'Consortium' has the same meaning as in 4.37 above. [*FA 1980, 10 Sch 26(5)*].

4.51 The close company legislation applies for the purpose of the provision in 4.50 above with the following amendments.

(*a*) There is a relaxation of the normal rules where a participant in an approved savings-related share option scheme is also a beneficiary under an employee trust holding shares in the company, e.g. an approved profit sharing scheme. No other beneficiary of such a trust is treated as an associate of the participant unless that other beneficiary and his relatives own, or could acquire as a result of the working of the trust, more than 25% of the company's ordinary share capital. [*FA 1980, 10 Sch 26(3)(b)*]. Under the normal close company rules, the figure of 5% would have to be substituted for 25% above.

(*b*) A person is only treated as having a 'material interest' in a company if he owns or can control more than 25% of the ordinary share capital or if more than 25% of the company's distributable income could be apportioned to him. [*ICTA 1970, s 285(6); FA 1980, 10 Sch 26(2)*]. Again, the figure of 5% would have to be substituted for 25% under the normal close company rules.

(*c*) The term 'close company' here includes any company not resident in the UK which would be close if it were so resident and any company which would be close but for the fact that some of its shares are quoted on a recognised stock exchange. [*FA 1980, 10 Sch 23(2)*].

4.52 It should be noted that the rules discussed above merely specify the limits as to who may participate. It is permissible to include others, e.g. those with less than five years' qualifying service, those who do not work full-time and those whose earnings are assessed under Schedule E, Case II or III. However, if people in these categories decide to participate, they must do so on similar terms to all other participants (see 4.45–4.46 above). On the other hand, there is no need for all eligible directors and employees actually to participate in a scheme. An individual's decision will obviously depend on his assessment of his company's prospects. It is possible that, when the date for exercise of the option arrives, the share price will have fallen and there will be no point in exercising the option. (Even if this happens, the SAYE scheme remains a method of saving which has attractions in its own right.)

Transfer of options

4.53 Options must not be transferable except that they must pass to a participant's personal representatives on his death (see 4.28 above). [*FA 1980, 10 Sch 11*].

Income tax and capital gains tax

4.54 Where a director or employee acquires and exercises a share option under an approved savings-related share option scheme, no income tax will normally be charged

(*a*) on the grant of the option; or

(*b*) if the option is exercised in accordance with the rules of the scheme at a time when it is an approved scheme, on the exercise of the option; or

(*c*) on any subsequent growth in the value of the shares.

[*FA 1980, s 47(1)*].

Thus, with one possible exception (see 4.55 below), the income tax charges which might otherwise apply to a participant are normally excluded where the scheme has Inland Revenue approval.

4.55 The one possible exception is *FA 1976, s 67*, which treats a director or higher-paid employee who acquires shares at an undervalue as having the benefit of an interest-free loan (see 2.64–2.68 above). If that provision were to apply, a participant would be treated as having the benefit of a loan equal to the difference between the market value of the shares acquired on the exercise of an option and the price actually paid for them. It is understood that the Revenue do not take this point in practice, and it is arguable that the wording of the legislation is wide enough to exclude *section 67* anyway.

4.56 There is one case in which the exemptions described in 4.54 above do not apply. This is where an option is exercised within three years of grant under a provision in the scheme permitting early exercise in any of the circumstances described in 4.34 above. [*FA 1980, s 47(2)*]. Such a provision may, but need not, be included in a scheme (see 4.34 above).

4.57 When scheme shares are disposed of the participant will be liable to capital gains tax (subject to the annual exemption). His base cost will be his actual outlay; there is no increase to market value. [*FA 1980, s 47(1)(b); FA 1981, s 90(3); FA 1984, s 39(1)*].

Example 3

4.58 On 1 July 1981 James and John were both granted options over 3,000 shares in A plc. The options are exercisable on 1 July 1986. At the time of grant of the options the shares were worth £1 each, but when the options are exercised they are worth £4 each. The price at which the options could be exercised was 90p a share. James' option was granted under an approved scheme, John's was not. Their respective positions are as follows.

	James	John
	£	£
Market value 1.7.86	12,000	12,000
Exercise price (90p × 3,000)	2,700	2,700
Gain	£9,300	£ 9,300
Assessable, *ICTA 1970, s 186*	NIL	£ 9,300
'Cost' for capital gains tax	£2,700	£12,000

4.59 In the case of exercise within three years of grant, all the normal income tax provisions apply. This may include the reinstatement of an income tax charge on the grant of the option, under *FA 1972, s 77* (see 2.7 above). Strictly, the charge is on the full value at the time of grant of the shares which may be obtained by exercising the option, less the price payable for them. This seems anomalous, since in fact the option will be exercised in part only (see 4.36 above). It is understood that the Revenue practice is not to reopen past years but to charge the gain actually realised under *ICTA 1970, s 186* in the year of exercise of the option. This seems a reasonable approach.

SAYE contracts

4.60 As has been seen, the scheme shares must be acquired with the proceeds of a SAYE contract. Since the price paid for the shares must not exceed the repayment actually made under the SAYE scheme (see 4.21 above), a participant must strictly speaking terminate his SAYE contract before exercising an option. Thus the holder of a five-year option cannot pay for his shares out of his own pocket while retaining his SAYE contract to obtain the seven-year bonus. Conversely, the holder of a seven-year option is unlikely to be able to terminate this SAYE contract after five years, reinvest the money and then exercise his option. The Board are understood to be reluctant to approve a scheme unless it provides that an option is to lapse if a participant obtains his SAYE repayment before the option is exercisable.

4.61 All participants must use SAYE contracts approved by the Board. In practice this means either the Department for National Savings (DNS) Fourth Issue of Save As You Earn contracts or the building societies' SAYE Share-save contracts.

The DNS Fourth Issue of Save As You Earn and the building societies' SAYE Share-save contracts are available to anyone aged 16 or over who is entitled to purchase scheme shares. Under these savings contracts the saver agrees to pay either to the DNS or to any building society in the scheme a fixed regular monthly sum between £10 and £100 over a five-year period normally by deduction from pay.

Under DNS contracts, contributions by monthly paid employees should be remitted to the SAYE Office each month, but where employees are weekly paid the amount deducted should be one quarter of the monthly contribution, to be remitted to the SAYE Office or to the building society concerned.

At the end of five years the 60 contributions made by a participant are payable to him on application together with a bonus equal to 14 monthly contributions. Alternatively, if repayment is not claimed for a further two years, the bonus becomes an amount equal to 28 monthly contributions. When the employee wants to withdraw the money he has to apply to DNS Durham or to the building society as appropriate.

If repayment is taken before the first anniversary no interest will be payable. But compound interest at the rate of 6% per annum will be payable on uncompleted contracts repaid between the first and fifth anniversaries. If repayment is taken between the fifth and seventh anniversaries compound interest at 6% per annum will be payable on the amount due at the fifth anniversary (including bonus) for the period between the fifth anniversary and the month of repayment.

A participant who leaves the company may, by arrangement with the DNS or with the building society concerned, continue to make monthly payments to his SAYE contract by a different method of payment.

Any bonus or interest payable is free of income tax.

4.62 There are transitional provisions to deal with savings schemes in existence before 15 November 1980. The effect of those provisions is that a certified contractual savings scheme used for the purpose of an unapproved savings-related share option scheme can be treated as if it were an approved SAYE scheme and can thus be used to fund the acquisition of shares under an approved savings-related share option scheme. However the amount of the proceeds which can be used in this way is restricted to the amount that would have been available if the terms of the scheme had been the same as those of an approved SAYE scheme. [*FA 1980, 10 Sch 24*]. Thus, within limits, savings accumulated before 1980 can be used for the purposes of a *Finance Act 1980* scheme.

Information

4.63 The Board may require any person to supply, within not less than thirty days, such information as they consider necessary for the purposes of these provisions. In particular, they may call for

(*a*) information to determine whether to approve a scheme, or to withdraw an approval previously given;

(*b*) information relating to the administration of a scheme and to any alterations in its terms; and

(*c*) information to determine the tax liability of any participant in a scheme.

[*FA 1980, 10 Sch 25*].

There are the normal penalties for failure to comply with a notice to supply such information. [*TMA 1970, s 98; FA 1980, s 121*].

4.64 Any company running a savings-related share option scheme will be required to submit annual returns to Technical Division (Employee Share Schemes). The returns will include particulars of options granted and of shares issued under the scheme.

Chapter 5

Approved Selective Share Option Schemes

Outline

5.1 The approved selective share option scheme introduced by the *Finance Act 1984* is an important step in encouraging share ownership by directors and employees. A number of features of this new scheme are likely to give it the widest interest. It offers probably the best available way of enabling senior management to acquire a significant slice of a company's equity in a tax-effective manner with a minimum of delay.

5.2 In outline, the new scheme is very simple. Selected directors and employees are granted options over scheme shares without payment or for a nominal sum. Generally speaking, the price at which the option can be exercised must not be less than the market price of those shares when the option is granted. This price must be stated at the time. The holders of the options are free to exercise them at the stated price within the time limits laid down by the rules of the scheme.

5.3 The new scheme is highly flexible. Broadly speaking, only full-time directors and employees are eligible to join. But the scheme can be used selectively, at the company's discretion. It need not be open to all full-time directors and staff. This will undoubtedly be seen as a major advantage by many employers.

5.4 The new scheme also caters for shareholding on a much bigger scale than either of the older types of approved scheme. Any director or employee can acquire options over shares worth up to £100,000. And there is an alternative higher limit of four times the current year's salary (or preceding year's salary if greater). So a man earning over £25,000 is eligible to acquire options over shares worth more than £100,000. Furthermore, as his salary rises from year to year so does his option limit. Obviously these are maximum figures and a company can specify its own lower ceiling if it wishes.

5.5 In a close company, the limits may be more restrictive. A director or employee is not eligible to be granted or to exercise options if he already holds more than 10% of the ordinary share capital.

5.6 The shares over which the options are granted must form part of the ordinary share capital of the employing company, of its parent company or, in some cases, of a member of a consortium owning the employing company or its parent. The shares may be quoted or unquoted, but shares in an unquoted subsidiary do not qualify unless the ultimate parent company is quoted. This means that a scheme for, say, employees of a trading subsidiary in an unquoted group is likely to involve the shares of the parent company.

5.7 The main tax privilege which approved selective share option schemes enjoy is freedom from the income tax liability which may arise under an unapproved scheme when options are granted or when they are exercised or both. Since the amounts involved may be substantial, this privilege is extremely valuable. The schemes also enjoy exemption from the income tax liability that may arise on the growth in the value of director and employee held shares.

5.8 However, to benefit from these tax privileges, an option holder must exercise his options not less than three or more than ten years after grant. And he must allow at least three years between each occasion on which an option is exercised.

5.9 Suppose the holder of an option over 100,000 shares decides to take up 50,000 of those shares after three years. He must wait another three years before he can exercise the option over the remaining shares tax-free. And if, three years later, he only takes up 25,000 shares, he has to wait yet another three years before he can acquire the balance without having to pay tax.

5.10 On exercising the option, the director or employee will need to find the money to purchase the shares. Even where the price per share is comparatively low, the total amount involved may be significant. Generally speaking, interest on a loan taken out to purchase such shares will qualify for tax relief provided that

(*a*) the company is close;

(*b*) it is a trading company or member of a trading group; and

(*c*) the shareholder is a director or senior executive.

[*FA 1972, s 75(1); FA 1974, s 19(1), 1 Sch 9(1), 10(1); FA 1982, s 49(2)–(4)*].

In cases where interest relief is not available there will generally be a ready market in the shares. Thus an immediate sale of part of the holding could be used to fund the purchase of the remaining shares (and the capital gains tax on the shares sold). It will be for the director or employee to weigh the merits of partial realisation against those of borrowing without tax relief.

5.11 Once the director or employee has exercised his options he is free to do what he likes with his shares, and if he sells them he will only be liable to capital gains tax.

Who may establish a scheme

5.12 Any body corporate may establish a selective share option scheme and obtain approval under these provisions. [*FA 1984, 10 Sch 1(1)*]. The body establishing the scheme need not be incorporated or resident in the UK. And, if it is incorporated in the UK, it need not be a company formed under the Companies Acts. It may, for instance, be a chartered company. However, it must be in a position to establish a scheme complying with the rules described in this chapter. It must be able, inter alia, to grant its directors and employees options over shares satisfying the conditions described in 5.37 to 5.42 below. And, unless at least some of the individuals participating in the scheme are within the UK tax net, there will be little point in going to the trouble of obtaining Revenue approval.

Scope of schemes

5.13 In many cases, the benefits of a selective share option scheme will be restricted to the directors and employees of the company which has established it. But where the company running such a scheme is the parent company of a group, the scheme may extend to the directors and employees of any of its subsidiaries. A scheme for a parent company and its subsidiaries is known as a 'group scheme', and any company which is included in the scheme (there is no need to include every company in the group) is referred to as a 'participating company'. For this purpose, a subsidiary is any company over which the parent has control. 'Control' has the meaning given in *ICTA 1970, s 534*. [*FA 1984, 10 Sch 1(3)(4), 15(1)*].

5.14 It is possible that a parent company which is in turn under the control of another company could establish a group scheme to extend to the directors and employees of its subsidiaries. But this scheme could not extend to the directors and employees of its holding company. This subject is discussed in 3.16 above, where there is an example illustrating a group scheme.

Approval procedure

5.15 A company which has established a selective share option scheme may apply to the Board for approval. The application must be in writing and must contain such information and be supported by such evidence as the Board may require. [*FA 1984, 10 Sch 1(1)(2)*]. There is no special form of application, but the following information should be provided.

(*a*) The name and registered office of the company which has established the scheme, the tax district to which it makes its returns and its reference number in that district. This information is also required for the company whose shares are to be subject to the options if that is not the company which has established the scheme, and, in the case of a 'group scheme' (see 5.13 above), for all companies to which the scheme extends.

(*b*) The memorandum and articles of association of the company whose shares are to be used, and any amendments.

(*c*) The rules of the scheme.

(*d*) The form of contract under which the option is to be granted.

(*e*) A declaration by the company which has established the scheme that the shares to be used satisfy the conditions in 5.37–5.42 below; a statement signed by the company secretary will suffice.

(*f*) If the shares which are to be subject to the options are not shares in the company which has established the scheme or are shares in a company which is under the control of another company, a further declaration indicating precisely how the conditions in 5.37–5.42 below are met.

(*g*) Any other documents which will be issued to participants or shareholders in connection with the scheme, including the option certificate and notice of exercise.

The application should state the date the scheme was approved or adopted by the company and, where the scheme has been subsequently amended, the date on which and by whom it was amended to its current form.

5.16 Applications for approval should be addressed to: Inland Revenue, Technical Division (Employee Share Schemes), Somerset House, London WC2R 1LB.

5.17 Share option schemes already in existence can be submitted for approval but will almost certainly need to be amended to comply with the statutory requirements. Only share options granted after 5 April 1984 qualify for the tax exemptions discussed in 5.50 and 5.53 below.

5.18 Generally speaking, options must not be granted until approval has been obtained. This will often involve a degree of delay. It was expected that, in the early part of 1985, the delay would be considerable. Therefore where an application for approval was submitted before 1 January 1985 any option granted before 1 July 1985 was treated as granted under an approved scheme provided that approval was subsequently obtained. There was no need to wait for approval before granting options in such cases. [*FA 1984, 10 Sch 1(5)*].

5.19 The legislation envisages that approval will be obtained only after a scheme has been drawn up and adopted by a company. There is no provision for the company to obtain advance confirmation that the terms of a scheme which it proposes to establish will qualify. A common procedure is to adopt a scheme and then amend the rules if need be in order to obtain approval. In addition, it is understood that the Technical Division (Employee Share Schemes) is prepared to comment informally on draft documentation and to discuss particular points of difficulty in advance of a formal application for approval.

5.20 The Board do not have any discretion with regard to the approval of selective share option schemes. They are obliged to approve a scheme provided that it meets the requirements listed at 5.24 below and does not include 'features . . . which are neither essential nor reasonably incidental' to its purpose of providing shares for directors and employees. [*FA 1984, 10 Sch 1(1)*]. A provision allowing the payment of cash in lieu of shares would violate this condition.

5.21 Any alteration to an approved scheme, however minor, must itself be approved by the Board, or the scheme as a whole will automatically lose its approved status from the date the alteration is adopted. [*FA 1984, 10 Sch 2(2)*]. This is an important point which can all too easily be overlooked in practice. It is therefore advisable to include in the rules of the scheme a provision that no alteration is to be made without the Board's prior approval.

5.22 Even where there is no alteration to a scheme the Board may if they see fit withdraw their approval if

(*a*) any of the conditions listed at 5.24 below is no longer met; or

(*b*) the company fails to provide any information requested by the Board under the provisions described in 5.61 below.

[*FA 1984, 10 Sch 2(1)*].

For the position where a participant who has obtained an option prior to the withdrawal of approval exercises it after that withdrawal, see 5.56 below.

5.23 Where the Board

(*a*) refuses to approve a scheme; or

(*b*) refuses to approve an alteration; or

(*c*) withdraws an approval previously given,

the company may appeal to the Special Commissioners within 30 days of notification. [*FA 1984, 10 Sch 3*]. It should be noted that the participants, who may be most seriously affected by the Board's decision, do not have any right of appeal.

Conditions for approval

5.24 If it is to obtain approval a scheme must satisfy a number of conditions. These are discussed below under the following main headings

(*a*) general conditions (see 5.25 below);

(*b*) monetary limits (see 5.26–5.31 below);

(*c*) the option price (see 5.32–5.33 below);

(*d*) the dates when options may be exercised (see 5.34–5.36 below);

(*e*) conditions relating to the scheme shares (see 5.37–5.42 below);

(*f*) conditions relating to the participants (see 5.43–5.48 below); and

(*g*) conditions relating to the transfer of options (see 5.49 below).

General

5.25 In general terms, the scheme must provide for directors and employees ('the participants') to obtain options to acquire shares which comply with the conditions described in 5.37–5.42 below ('the scheme shares'). The scheme shares have to be paid for out of the participant's own pocket. [*FA 1984, 10 Sch 6*].

Monetary limit

5.26 The rules of the scheme must impose a limit on the value of the shares over which any one director or employee may obtain options at any one time. This limit must apply so that the total value of shares for which options are held under the scheme itself, and under any other scheme established by the same or an associated company (within the meaning of *ICTA 1970, s 302*) and approved under the provisions of the *Finance Act 1984*, does not exceed the limit stated in 5.28 below. [*FA 1984, 10 Sch 5(1)*].

5.27 For the purpose of calculating the limit, the value of shares is to be taken as their market value at the time when the relevant option is granted, unless the Board have agreed to use the value at some earlier time, as described in 5.32 below. [*FA 1984, 10 Sch 5(4)*]. Subsequent fluctuations in the share value do not affect this calculation.

5.28 The limit on the value of shares under unexercised options is the greatest of

(*a*) £100,000; or

(*b*) four times the employee's remuneration for the year of assessment in which options are to be granted; or

(*c*) four times his remuneration for the preceding year of assessment; or

(*d*) where there was no remuneration for the preceding year of assessment, e.g. because the employment started in the current year, four times the remuneration for the twelve months beginning with the first day on which remuneration was earned.

[*FA 1984, 10 Sch 5(2)(3)*].

5.29 For this purpose, remuneration means earnings from the office or employment entitling the individual to participate in the scheme. Only remuneration from which income tax must be deducted under PAYE may be taken into account. Benefits in kind and reimbursed expenses are to be ignored. [*FA 1984, 10 Sch 5(5)*]. Earnings qualifying for the 100% deduction for long absences abroad also appear strictly speaking to be excluded from the calculation; but it is to be hoped that the Revenue would adopt a more liberal approach to overseas earnings in practice.

Example 1

5.30 John Smith's income as a director of Smith & Jones plc is as follows.

		1984/85		1985/86
		£		£
Salary		20,000		24,000
Bonus		10,000		5,000
Car benefit	750		825	
Fuel benefit	750		825	
Golf club subscription	120	1,620	150	1,800
		£31,620		£30,800

His maximum entitlement in 1985/86 is

4 × (£20,000 + £10,000) = £120,000

5.31 Where remuneration falls, for instance owing to fluctuating bonus payments, an option may be within the limit when granted but may be in excess of the limit in a subsequent year. This will not disqualify existing options but will preclude the granting of new options until remuneration rises again, establishing a new, higher limit.

Option price

5.32 The price at which an option obtained under a selective share option scheme may be exercised must be stated at the time when that option is granted. It must not be manifestly less than the market value of shares of that class at that time, or at such earlier time (not normally more than 30 days before the grant of the option) as the Board and the company agree in writing. However, provision may be made to vary the stated price to take account of any variations in the company's share capital, e.g. bonus issues or rights issues. [*FA 1984, 10 Sch 13*]. It will be appreciated that these provisions merely lay down a minimum price at which options may be exercised under an approved scheme. There is no objection to setting the price higher and indeed in many cases this may be considered appropriate.

5.33 Where the shares are quoted, the market value at the time of the grant of the option will be easy to ascertain. Where the shares are not quoted, the market value will have to be agreed with the Inland Revenue's Share Valuation Division.

Date of exercise of option

5.34 The legislation contains no requirements about exercise dates as a condition of approval of a scheme. It merely provides that the various tax exemptions (see 5.53 below) will be available if an option is exercised:

(*a*) not less than three or more than ten years after grant; and

(*b*) not less than three years after the participant last exercised an option under an approved scheme.

[*FA 1984, s 38(3)(4)*].

5.35 However, where a scheme permits an option holder's personal representatives to exercise an option within one year of his death (see 5.54 below), the tax exemptions will apply provided that the exercise occurs less than ten years after the option was granted. In other words, the exemptions will be available even if the exercise occurs less than three years after the grant of the option or less than three years after the last exercise of an option under an approved scheme by the deceased. [*FA 1984, 10 Sch 12(2)*].

5.36 There are no special rules to cater for amalgamations and reconstructions. There are, for instance, no provisions to deal with cases where the company whose shares are used in the scheme is taken over within three years of the grant of options and thus before those options can be exercised tax free. If the rules of the scheme permit, any participant who wishes to do so may exercise his options in advance of the takeover, but he will suffer the normal income tax charges. There is no exemption where an option is exercised within three years of grant in these circumstances.

The shares

5.37 The scheme shares must form part of the ordinary share capital of:

(*a*) the company which established the scheme; or

(*b*) a company having control of the company which established the scheme; or

(*c*) a company which is a member of a consortium owning either the company in (*a*) or the company in (*b*) and which itself owns beneficially not less than 15% of the consortium company in question; or

(*d*) a company which has control of the consortium member in (*c*).

[*FA 1984, 10 Sch 7*].

'Control' has the meaning given in *ICTA 1970, s 534*. [*FA 1984, 10 Sch 15(1)*]. A company is a member of a consortium owning another company if it is one of a number of companies owning between them not less than 75% of the other company's ordinary share capital and each owning not less than 5% of that ordinary share capital. [*FA 1984, 10 Sch 15(4)*]. 'Ordinary share capital' has the meaning given in *ICTA 1970, s 526(5)*, and thus includes participating preference shares.

5.38 The scheme shares must be

(*a*) quoted shares; or

(*b*) unquoted shares in a company which is not under the control of any other company; or

(*c*) unquoted shares in a company which is under the control of a quoted company (other than a quoted company which is, or would if resident in the UK be, a close company).

'Control' has the meaning given in *ICTA 1970, s 534*. [*FA 1984, 10 Sch 8, 15(1)*].

Thus a scheme for, say, directors and employees of a trading subsidiary in an unquoted group is likely to rely on the shares of the parent company. The shares of the trading subsidiary cannot be scheme shares. It is apparently considered that the profits of a subsidiary can too easily be manipulated to the benefit or detriment of employee shareholders.

5.39 The shares must be fully paid up, must not be redeemable, and must not be subject to any restrictions not attaching to all shares of the same class, with the following exception.

It is permissible for the company's articles of association to require that all shares held by directors and employees be sold on cessation of employment; and, where a share option is exercised after employment has ceased, the articles may require that the shares be sold immediately after acquisition. However, the articles must require that the shares be sold for cash, and must prescribe the terms of sale. What is more, these terms must apply to all holders of shares of the same class, not just to directors and employees. In other words, the terms of sale must form part of general disposal provisions. [*FA 1984, 10 Sch 9; FA 1986, s 22(3)(4)*].

5.40 For this purpose, the term 'restriction' includes any contract, agreement, arrangement or condition which

(*a*) limits a person's freedom to dispose of his shares, of any interest in them or of the proceeds of their sale; or

(*b*) limits his freedom to exercise any right conferred by those shares; or

(*c*) might make such a disposal or exercise disadvantageous to him or to any person connected with him.

[*FA 1984, 10 Sch 10(1)*].

'Connected person' here has the meaning given in *ICTA 1970, s 533*.

5.41 However, restrictions similar to those in the Stock Exchange 'Model Code for Securities Transactions by Directors of Listed Companies' issued in November 1984 will be ignored. [*FA 1984, 10 Sch 10(2); FA 1986, s 23(4)*].

5.42 If the company has more than one class of ordinary share capital, the majority of the shares of the class to which the scheme shares belong must *either* be 'employee-control shares' *or* be held by persons other than

(*a*) persons who acquired their shares in pursuance of a right conferred on them or an opportunity afforded to them as directors or employees; or

(*b*) trustees for such shareholders (e.g. the trustees of an approved profit sharing scheme); or

(*c*) in the case of unquoted shares, any company which controls the company whose shares are scheme shares or of which that company is an associated company. [*FA 1984, 10 Sch 11*]. 'Associated company' has the meaning given in *ICTA 1970, s 302*.

'Employee-control shares' are shares held by present or former directors or employees of the company or of a company it controls who together are able, as holders of those shares, to control the company in question.

The participants

5.43 The scheme must provide that options shall only be granted to or exercised by full-time directors or qualifying employees of the company or, in the case of a group scheme, of one of the participating companies. [*FA 1984, 10 Sch 4(1)(a)*]. The term 'full-time director' is not defined in the legislation, but the Revenue have stated that they consider a 'full-time director' is one who works at least 25 hours a week. A 'qualifying employee' is one who is obliged to work at least 20 hours a week. [*FA 1984, 10 Sch 15(1)*]. The minimum hours of work quoted above both for directors and for employees exclude meal breaks. For the purpose of these tests, a person may aggregate the hours he works for all participating companies in a group scheme (see 5.13 above).

5.44 In spite of the rule restricting participation to current directors and employees, a scheme may, if desired, provide that

(*a*) where a person ceases to be a full-time director or qualifying employee before exercising an option, he may exercise it subsequently [*FA 1984, 10 Sch 4(2)*]; and

(*b*) where a director or employee dies without having exercised an option, his personal representatives may exercise it within one year of his death. [*FA 1984, 10 Sch 12*].

5.45 The approved selective share option scheme is not designed to enable directors or employees to obtain a substantial interest in a close company, and there are provisions to ensure that the schemes cannot be used for this purpose. Thus a scheme must not permit an option to be granted to, or exercised by, a person if he has, or in the preceding twelve months has had, a 'material interest' in a 'close company' which is (*a*) the company whose shares are to be scheme shares; or

(*b*) a company controlling that company or a member of a consortium owning that company.

[*FA 1984, 10 Sch 4(1)(b)*].

In determining whether a person has a material interest in a company, the interests of his associates must be taken into account. 'Consortium' has the same meaning as in 5.37 above. [*FA 1984, 10 Sch 15(4)*].

5.46 The close company legislation applies for the purpose of the provision in 5.45 above with the following amendments.

(*a*) There is a relaxation of the normal rules where a participant in an approved selective share option scheme is also a beneficiary under an employee trust holding shares in the company, e.g. an approved profit sharing scheme. No other beneficiary of such a trust is treated as an associate of the participant unless that other beneficiary and his relatives own, or could acquire as a result of the working of the trust, more than 10% of the company's ordinary share capital. [*FA 1984, 10 Sch 4(4), 15(2)*]. Under the normal close company rules, the figure of 5% would have to be substituted for 10% above.

(*b*) A person is only treated as having a 'material interest' in a company if he owns or can control more than 10% of the ordinary share capital or if more than 10% of the company's distributable income could be apportioned to him. [*ICTA 1970, s 285(6); FA 1984, 10 Sch 4(4)*]. Again, the figure of 5% would have to be substituted for 10% under the normal close company rules.

(*c*) The term 'close company' here includes any company not resident in the UK which would be close if it were so resident and any company which would be close but for the fact that some of its shares are quoted on a recognised stock exchange. [*FA 1984, 10 Sch 4(3)*].

5.47 It has been seen that an individual has a material interest in a company if more than 10% of the company's distributable income could be apportioned to him or to his associates. This apportionment is based on 'the respective interests in the company in question of the participators'. [*FA 1972, 16 Sch 4(2)*]. Anyone who holds an option is a participator even if he holds no shares in the company. [*ICTA 1970, s 303(1)*]. It is therefore clear that shares under option must be taken into account in determining whether an individual has a material interest. What is less clear is the basis on which they enter into the calculation. The Revenue view is that they rank pari passu with shares already in issue. It may be doubted whether a valuation of an option holder's interest would justify this approach, but assuming it to be correct prospective participants fall into two categories, as follows.

(*a*) Those who already have a material interest in a company are not eligible for the grant of options.

(*b*) Those who do not already have a material interest are eligible, even if the new options will result in the recipient having a material interest.

A person who has a material interest cannot exercise any options, even though they were properly acquired. He may, however, subsequently cease to have a material interest (e.g. by disposing of part of his holding, or through an increase in the total share capital or options in issue) and will then be eligible to exercise options.

Example 2

5.48 The authorised share capital of Henry Fielding & Sons Limited is 10,000 ordinary shares of £1 each, of which 9,000 are in issue. 500 shares are held by Tom Jones. His son Dick holds no shares at present but is managing director of the company and is granted an option over 1,000 shares under an approved selective share option scheme. Once the option has been granted, Dick Jones has a material interest in Henry Fielding & Sons Limited because, taking account of

(*a*) the shares under option to him, and

(*b*) the shares owned by an associate (his father),

more than 10% of the company's distributable income could (on the Revenue's view) be apportioned to him. Dick Jones will not be entitled to exercise his option unless, for instance, his father disposes of his 500 shares. Even then he will have to wait a year before exercising the option.

Transfer of options

5.49 The rules of the scheme must provide that options are not transferable. [*FA 1984, 10 Sch 12(1)*]. The position on the death of an option holder is discussed in 5.35 above.

Income tax

5.50 A director or employee who is granted an option under an approved scheme is not liable to income tax on the occasion of the grant unless there is an element of discount in the price at which the option may be exercised. [*FA 1984, s 38(2)*]. Where a discount is present it will be assessed under Schedule E for the year of assessment in which the option is granted. The assessment is on the excess of the market value of the shares at the time of the grant over the sum of

(*a*) the price, if any, paid for the option; and

(*b*) the price at which the shares may be purchased.

[*FA 1984, s 38(5)*].

The assessment is not made under the provisions of *FA 1972, s 77*, and a liability may arise even if an option cannot be exercised more than seven years after it is granted.

5.51 Bearing in mind that

(*a*) it is a condition of approval of a scheme that the price at which options may be exercised is not less than the market value of shares of the relevant class at the time of grant, or at such earlier time (not normally more than 30 days before the time of grant) as the Board and the company agree in writing, and

(*b*) the Revenue have indicated that the provision discussed in 5.50 above will not be used to deal with fluctuations in the value of unquoted shares over the 30 days following agreement of a price by the Share Valuation Division,

it seems that the provision will operate only where, as a result of an unintentional breach of the rules, an option is granted with an exercise price which turns out to be less than the market value eventually agreed.

Example 3

5.52 On 1 January 1986 A Ltd grants to its employee B an option to acquire 1,000 ordinary shares at a price of £9 per share, exercisable between 1 January 1992 and 31 December 1992. The market value per share at 1 January 1986 is subsequently agreed at £10, but a value of £9 had been agreed with the Board at 1 November 1985. B paid £100 for the option. A discount of £900 will be assessed under Schedule E for 1985/86 calculated as follows.

	£	£
Market value of 1,000 shares in A Ltd at 31 December 1985		10,000
Cost of option	100	
Exercise price	9,000	
		9,100
Assessable under Sch E		£900

5.53 A participant who exercises an option in accordance with the rules of an approved scheme will not be liable to income tax on the exercise of the option or on any subsequent appreciation in the value of the shares provided that the date of exercise is

(*a*) not less than three or more than ten years after grant; and

(*b*) not less than three years after his last exercise of an option under the same or any other approved scheme.

There is no objection to a participant exercising more than one option on the same day, whether or not under the same approved scheme. [*FA 1984, s 38(3)(4)*].

5.54 The only case in which three years' delay is not required before the tax free exercise of an option is where the scheme permits a participant's personal representatives to exercise an option within one year of his death (see 5.35 above).

Example 4

5.55 A participant is granted options under an approved selective share option scheme as follows.

Option	Date of grant	No of shares
1	31 October 1985	1,000
2	10 October 1986	1,100
3	1 November 1987	1,250
4	21 October 1988	1,400
5	15 October 1989	1,500

The participant may exercise option 1 tax free on 1 November 1988. If he does so, the first date on which he may exercise options 2, 3 and 4 tax free is 1 November 1991. Assuming he adopts this exercise date, he must wait until 1 November 1994 before exercising option 5 without incurring an income tax liability.

5.56 If approval of the scheme has been withdrawn by the time the option is exercised, the director or employee will face an income tax assessment under Schedule E on the excess of the market value of the shares at the time of acquisition over the sum of

(*a*) the price, if any, paid for the option; and

(*b*) the price at which the shares were purchased.

This assessment, which arises under the provisions of *ICTA 1970, s 186* (see 2.12 above), is reduced to take account of any discount assessed when the option was granted. [*FA 1984, s 38(7)(a)(8)*].

Example 5

5.57 The facts are the same as in Example 3 above. On 1 April 1992 B exercises the option, but by this time the approval for the scheme has been withdrawn. The market value of the shares on 1 April 1992 is £20,000. A gain of £10,000 will be assessed under Schedule E for 1991/92 calculated as follows.

	£	£
Market value of shares at 1.4.92		20,000
Cost of option	100	
Acquisition price	9,000	
		9,100
		10,900
Less: Discount assessed 1985/86		900
Assessable under Sch E		£10,000

5.58 Since an assessment under *ICTA 1970, s 186* can be made only where the earnings from the directorship or employment by reason of which the option was granted are assessed under Schedule E, Case I, the provisions of *FA 1976, s 67* (see 2.64 above) may apply to participants assessed under Schedule E, Case II or Case III. If such a participant exercises an option after the approval for a scheme has been withdrawn, the difference between the market value of the shares and the price paid for them will be treated as an interest-free loan from the company and may give rise to an assessable benefit. The notional loan is reduced by such a proportion of the discount as is attributable to the shares in question. [*FA 1984, s 38(7)(b)(9)*].

Capital gains tax

5.59

Where, as will usually be the case, the exercise of the option does not give rise to any income tax liability, the acquisition cost of the shares for capital gains tax purposes will be the sum of

(i) any amount paid for the grant of the option; and

(ii) the price actually paid for the shares (not the market value at the time of acquisition) [*FA 1984, s 38(3)(b)*]; and

(iii) the amount of any assessment on discount raised on the grant of the option (see 5.50 above). [*FA 1984, s 38(6)*].

Where a liability to income tax does arise on the exercise of the option, the capital gains tax cost will be increased by the amount on which income tax is chargeable. [*ICTA 1970, s 186(12)*].

If the option is allowed to lapse, the cost of the option is not allowable as a loss either for income tax or for capital gains tax. [*CGTA 1979, s 137(4)*].

Example 6

5.60 The facts are the same as in Example 5. The cost of B's shares for capital gains tax purposes is calculated as follows.

	£
Cost of option	100
Price paid for shares	9,000
Discount assessed, 1985/86	900
Sch E assessment, 1991/92	10,000
	£20,000

Information

5.61 The Board may require any person to supply such information as they consider necessary for the purposes of these provisions. [*FA 1984, 10 Sch 14*]. In particular, they may call for (*a*) information to determine whether to approve a scheme, or to withdraw an approval previously given;

(*b*) information relating to the administration of a scheme and to any alterations in its terms; and

(*c*) information to determine the tax liability of any participant in a scheme, including liability to capital gains tax.

A person can only be called upon to provide information which he has or can reasonably be expected to obtain, and must be given at least thirty days to reply.

5.62 There are the normal penalties for failure to comply with a notice under 5.61 above. [*TMA 1970, s 98; FA 1984, s 38(10)*].

Chapter 6

Company Law

6.1 This chapter outlines a small number of company law provisions which may have particular relevance to employee share schemes.

Adoption of scheme

6.2 The general authority for the issue of shares by a company excludes shares in an employee share scheme; and normally a scheme is adopted by resolution of the company in general meeting. In certain cases it may also be necessary to authorise the grant of options and/or the allotment of shares pursuant to the scheme. [*CA 1985, ss 80(1)(2), 87(1)*].

Disclosure

6.3 A director's interests in the company's shares, including share options, must be disclosed in the annual report or as a note to the accounts. [*CA 1985, s 235, 7 Sch 2*].

The requirement to disclose directors' emoluments would cover share options granted, shares acquired at an undervalue, etc. [*CA 1985, s 231, 5 Sch 22*].

Acquisition of assets by directors

6.4 There is a prohibition against purchases by directors of certain options in respect of issued shares in a listed company. However, there is an exemption from this prohibition where the director buys an option to subscribe for new shares. [*CA 1985, s 323*].

A company is prohibited from entering into an arrangement whereby a director is to acquire assets other than cash from the company. [*CA 1985, s 320(1)(a)*]. Non-cash assets include shares and share options. However, this prohibition does not apply if

(i) the value of the assets at the time the arrangement is made
- (*a*) is under £1,000; or
- (*b*) does not exceed the lesser of £50,000 and 10% of the company's net assets; or

(ii) the arrangement is approved by ordinary resolution of the company in general meeting.

[*CA 1985, s 320(2)*].

Provision of financial assistance

6.5 Subject to a number of exceptions, a company is prohibited from giving financial assistance, direct or indirect, for the acquisition of its own shares or of the shares of its holding company. [*CA 1985, s 151*].

This provision is not considered to affect share option schemes, which do not depend on financial assistance from the company as that expression is defined in this context. [*CA 1985, s 152*].

Furthermore, a company is permitted to provide finance for the acquisition of fully paid shares of the company or of its holding company in accordance with the rules of an employee share scheme such as an approved profit sharing scheme. A company is also permitted to make loans to employees (but in general not to directors; see 6.6 below) to enable them to acquire shares in the company or in its holding company. [*CA 1985, s 153(4)*].

Thus the prohibition of the provision of financial assistance is unlikely to affect share option or incentive schemes.

Loans to directors

6.6 A company is prohibited (with limited exceptions) from making loans to its directors. [*CA 1985, s 330*].

The main exceptions are

(i) loans not exceeding £2,500;

(ii) certain loans not exceeding £1,000 and repayable within two months; and

(iii) certain loans by money-lending companies.

[*CA 1985, s 332*].

It will be clear that a director will normally have to fund the acquisition of shares out of his own pocket.

Chapter 7

Investment Committee Guidelines

7.1 Subject to the statutory limits on participation by individuals (see 3.33–3.35, 4.22 and 5.26–5.31 above) a company is free to decide how many shares will be committed to share schemes for directors and employees. Here, the number of shares available may well prove the limiting factor. Companies with institutional investors (and in particular those with a full listing on The Stock Exchange) will need to take account of the guidelines issued by the investment committees.

7.2 These generally limit the number of shares issued or issuable under all the company's share schemes taken together over a ten-year period to 10% of the equity (5% if participation is restricted to the company's 'executives'). In addition, not more than 3% of the equity may normally be committed to the company's share schemes in any one calendar year, and within this total a maximum of 1% may be taken up under profit sharing schemes. The annual limit may be relaxed slightly in the year of introduction of a new scheme.

7.3 The Appendix contains the guidelines published by the investment committees of the Association of British Insurers and the National Association of Pension Funds Ltd.

Investment committee guidelines (reproduced by kind permission of the respective associations)

Association of British Insurers (April 1985)

SHARE OPTION AND PROFIT SHARING INCENTIVE SCHEMES "GUIDELINES" TO REQUIREMENTS OF INSURANCE OFFICES AS INVESTORS

The guidelines to share option and profit sharing schemes eligible for special taxation treatment under earlier legislation have been revised following the enactment of the Finance Act 1984 and the requirements set out below outline the restrictions insurance Offices regard as essential under such schemes if excessive appropriation of the equity entitlement of present shareholders is to be avoided.

In discharge of their responsibilities to policy holders and others on whose behalf they invest, insurance Offices have a duty to permit only those schemes which make available to participants such an appropriation of the profits and share capital of companies as is equitable having regard to the finance provided by the proprietors of the company in the past and their reasonable expectations of growth in the future. The Committee believes that the method of providing incentive arrangements in any company is a matter for the decision of its management and that directors will take account of all the interests concerned in formulating the particular schemes proposed which, in all cases, should be submitted to shareholders for approval. However, as judgement of the incentive effects of particular arrangements in individual companies is essentially a matter for its shareholders, it does not follow that observance of all the requirements set out below will necessarily ensure support for schemes which shareholders may feel are inappropriate on other grounds. The guidelines are intended merely to indicate the basic provisions necessary to give general effect to the principles outlined above in the hope that the scheme proposed will comply with the spirit as well as the letter of the requirements so as to ensure a genuine community of interest between shareholders and scheme beneficiaries. The main objective of the guidelines is to ensure that over a period of ten years not more than 10% of the shareholders' equity is utilised for schemes of all kinds. Furthermore, in order to conserve the benefits under such schemes for future participants, not more than 3% of the equity is appropriated for all forms of scheme in any three year period.

Accordingly, unless there are very exceptional circumstances, insurance Offices will be recommended to oppose proposals for the adoption of any scheme which does not satisfy each of the following requirements.

Profit Sharing Schemes

(1) The aggregate of the amount of the equity share capital of the proposing company that may be issued in any calendar year by way of subscription under profit sharing schemes may not exceed 1% of such share capital in issue on the day preceding the appropriation of profits for the purpose of the scheme as set out under Requirement (3).

(2) The aggregate of the amounts that may be appropriated out of profits in any calendar year for all profit sharing arrangements involving the acquisition of the company's shares may not exceed 5% of that proportion of the profits of the relevant trading period before tax and excluding exceptional items which, in the opinion of the directors, is attributable to the UK operations of the proposing company. Whenever the amount so appropriated would subscribe at the price calculated in accordance with Requirement (4) more than the amount of share capital permitted under Requirement (1), the balance of such appropriation may be applied in the purchase of shares in the market.

(3) The appropriation of profits for profit sharing schemes shall be made once only by the directors after announcement of the final results for the trading period in respect of which the appropriation is made and paid over to the trustees of the scheme as soon as practicable.

(4) The price at which shares are subscribed under Requirement (1) shall be the middle market price of the shares of the same class on the dealing day prior to the appropriation of profits under Requirement (3).

(5) On any occasion when part of the appropriation under Requirement (3) is applied in the purchase of shares in the market, the price at which shares are made available to participants under the scheme shall be the average per share of the cost of the shares subscribed under Requirement (4) and the cost including expenses of the shares purchased.

(6) Any monies received by the trustees for the acquisition of shares shall not be retained but shall be applied as far as practicable forthwith in the subscription or purchase of shares for immediate appropriation to the individuals eligible under the scheme.

(7) Any monies received by the trustees by way of dividends on the shares held in trust shall not be retained but shall be distributed immediately to the individual to whom the relevant shares have been appropriated.

(8) On any occasion when the voting rights attached to the shares held in trust fall to be exercised, the trustees shall obtain the instructions of the individuals to whom the relevant shares have been appropriated and exercise the voting rights accordingly.

Option Schemes

(9) Except as provided in (10) below, the amount of share capital issued or issuable under the scheme when aggregated with any share capital issued or issuable by the company under any other share option or profit sharing scheme within the preceding ten years must not exceed 10% of the equity share capital of the company at any time when a participation is granted except that where participation is restricted to "executives" of the company, 5% only of the equity share capital of the company is to be made available.

(10) In the case of a company having a market capitalisation of £5 millions or less, up to 10% of the equity capital when aggregated in accordance with (9) above may be issuable under the scheme provided that the market value of such capital does not exceed £500,000 at the time of the adoption of the scheme.

(11) The market value at the relevant time of the share capital to be appropriated, by allotment or by options granted, to any one participant when aggregated with the market value at the time of appropriation of any share capital appropriated in the preceding ten years to that participant under the proposed or previous option schemes must not exceed four times the participant's total annual emoluments from the companies within the scheme. In the case of schemes approved by the Inland Revenue under the Finance Act 1984 and which do not provide option linking arrangements, options granted up to 1st October 1979 under other schemes may, for the purpose of the individual participation limit, be disregarded and options granted under other schemes after 1st October 1979 but before the adoption of the proposed scheme may be taken into account at one half of the market value of the relevant shares at the date of the grant.

(12) The prices at which shares are issued to participants, or at which participants are given an option to subscribe, must not be less than the middle market price of the shares in question at the time when the participation is granted which must not precede and be within the 42 days following publication of the results of the grantor company.

(13) No option may be granted for more than ten years or exercised within three years of the date of the grant except that in the event of the take-over of the grantor company or the death or cessation of employment of the participant options must be exercised or lapse within one year or within three and one half years from the date of grant, whichever is the later. No option may be granted within the two years preceding the normal retirement date of the participant.

(14) Participation under the proposed scheme must be restricted to directors or employees who are required to devote substantially the whole of their working time to the business of the grantor company or its

subsidiaries and options, which must be non-assignable, may be granted only over the share capital of the grantor or its parent company.

Savings Related Schemes

(15) The proposed scheme must provide that in the period of ten years commencing at the date of its adoption the total amount of share capital issued or issuable under any savings related scheme when aggregated with the total amount of share capital issued or issuable under any other profit sharing or option scheme in the preceding ten years, whether or not approved under the Finance Acts, shall not exceed 10% of the equity share capital of the company at the time when capital is issued or issuable under the proposed scheme. "Issuable" share capital includes any share capital in respect of which options have been granted or rights may be exercised.

(16) Participation under the proposed scheme may be granted only within a period of ten years from the date of its adoption.

(17) The price at which participants are given an option to subscribe must not be less than the middle market price of the shares of the class under option at the time when the option is granted unless the scheme has received Inland Revenue approval under statutory provisions relating to contractual savings schemes in which event the option price must be not less than 90% of the middle market price.

(18) No part of the equity share capital may be issued or issuable to participants for subscription out of the proceeds of a contractual savings scheme except as provided under (15) above.

(19) The maximum amount that may be contracted for savings by individual participation under the scheme shall not exceed £150 per calendar month.

(20a) To conserve benefits for future participants all schemes must provide that not more than 3% of the equity capital may be appropriated for options or subscribed out of profits under all relevant schemes in any year and the two preceding years.

(20b) In the year of introduction of any scheme or schemes otherwise complying with all the above requirements the restriction under (20a) need not be observed provided that the percentage of equity capital appropriated for options or subscribed out of profits under all relevant schemes in that year and the four preceding years does not exceed 5% when a scheme available to employees generally is in operation or 3% when schemes are restricted to executives only.

The National Association of Pension Funds Limited (November 1984)

Covering letter

SHARE SCHEME GUIDELINES

The Investment Committee of the National Association of Pension Funds has reviewed its guidelines applicable to share schemes with the following three underlying objectives at the heart of its deliberations:

1. To limit the extent of total equity dilution arising from such schemes.
2. To prevent the permissible issue of shares being pre-empted by an excessively small group of individuals.
3. To ensure that such schemes involve an incentive for the recipients.

In setting out these new guidelines, which replace all previous guidelines issued by the NAPF, the Committee requests all companies proposing any share scheme to make a clear statement at the beginning of the appropriate documentation to shareholders that:

"The following proposals conform to the broad guidelines issued by the NAPF in November 1984",

or to state in what way a particular scheme does not conform and to explain to shareholders the company's justification for any non-conformity. A copy of the full final documentation should be sent to the NAPF Investment Committee and may be the subject of a check.

It is anticipated that companies will normally be able to make such a statement when proposing share schemes. NAPF members have been asked to make the secretariat aware of any schemes where such a disclosure is not made to shareholders.

In constructing the guidelines care has been taken to provide sufficient flexibility to permit all schemes to conform. The Committee regards as particularly important the willingness of companies to consider shareholders' interests by explaining in the documentation any unusual features of any scheme. It anticipates that companies not being willing to make such an explanatory disclosure to shareholders will be regarded with disfavour by its members, as will any significant breach of these guidelines.

Guidelines

SHARE SCHEME GUIDELINES

A. ALL SCHEMES IN AGGREGATE

1. The total number of voting and non-voting ordinary shares which may be issued or placed under option under all schemes in aggregate

(including non-approved, savings related and profit sharing schemes) during the preceding ten years may not exceed 10% of, and should be proportional to, the issued ordinary voting and non-voting share capital on the last working day before grant.

B. OPTION SCHEMES (Finance Act 1984 and unapproved)

2. Within (1) above, where the recipients are a restricted group (bearing in mind Paragraph 39(2) (ab) of the Finance Act 1984), not more than 5% of the number of issued ordinary shares may be made available to option schemes for such groups, in aggregate, over the relevant ten year period.

3. No option should be granted to any individual who is within 2 years of their normal anticipated retirement date.

4. No option may normally be exercised within three years from its date of grant; or later than 10 years from date of grant.

5. Options may only be cancelled or renounced by their holders within the first month after grant.

6. The prices at which shares are issued to participants, or at which participants are given an option to subscribe, must be not less than the middle market price of the shares in question at the time when participation is granted.

7. The limitations on the value of shares which may be allocated to an individual from time to time shall be those which permit qualification within the requirements of the Finance Act 1984 for taxation of the individual benefits at capital gains tax rates.

C. OTHER SCHEMES

Within the constraint of paragraph 1 above, the following additional guidelines specifically apply to savings related and profit sharing schemes.

8. Savings Related Schemes (Finance Act 1980)

(i) The maximum permissible monthly contribution by an individual is the lesser of the Inland Revenue limit and £150.

(ii) The exercise price for a share under option may not be less than 90% of the middle market price on the last dealing day before the date of grant.

9. Profit Sharing Schemes (Finance Act 1978)

(i) The aggregate of the amounts that may be appropriated out of profits in any calendar year for all profit sharing arrangements involving the acquisition of the company's shares may not, in aggregate, exceed 5% of that proportion of the profits of the relevant trading period (before tax and excluding exceptional items) which, in the opinion of the directors, is attributable to the UK operations of the proposing company.

(ii) Not more than 1% of the issued ordinary share capital may be subscribed in any one year for profit sharing schemes.

(iii) The price at which shares are subscribed shall be the middle market price of the shares of the same class on the dealing day prior to the appropriation of profits.

(iv) On any occasion when the voting rights attached to shares held in trust fall to be exercised, the trustees shall obtain the instructions of the individuals to whom the relevant shares have been appropriated and exercise the voting rights accordingly.

Index

A

Approved profit sharing scheme, 1.4, 1.5, 3
advantages, 3.13
alteration, 3.21
amalgamation, company, *see* company reconstruction
amount of contributions, 3.115
appropriate allowance, 3.76, 3.77
appropriate percentage, 3.67, 3.68, 3.76
appropriation of shares, 3.54, 3.59–3.62
approval
—alteration, 3.21, 3.23
—appeal, 3.23
—application, 3.17, 3.18
—conditions for, 3.20, 3.24–3.57
—prior discussion, 3.19
—procedure, 3.17–3.20, 3.23
—refusal, 3.23
—requirements, 3.20, 3.24–3.57
—withdrawal, 3.22, 3.23, 3.43
associate, 3.55, 3.56
associated company, 3.42
bankruptcy, trustee in, 3.47, 3.66
capital distribution, 3.80
capital gains tax, 3.99–3.104
—acquisition cost, 3.61, 3.71
—appropriation to participant, 3.61, 3.100, 3.101
—capital receipt, 3.80
—computation, 3.71
—identification of shares, 3.64, 3.102
—reconstruction, 3.45
—transfer to participant, 3.61
—trustees, 3.101, 3.102, 3.117, 3.120
—trustees' acts, 3.61, 3.66
capital receipts, 3.74–3.80
—capital gains tax, 3.80
—locked-in value calculation, 3.67
—meaning, 3.74, 3.75
—PAYE, 3.106, 3.107
—reconstruction, 3.84, 3.87, 3.88
—release date, before, 3.76–3.80
—unauthorised shares, 3.98
cash alternative, 3.20, 3.57
close company, 3.55, 3.56
company, *see also* group
—associated, 3.42
—close, 3.55, 3.56
—contribution by, 3.111, 3.115
—control, 3.15, 3.16, 3.36, 3.37, 3.45, 3.51
—control, change of, 3.45
—eligible to establish scheme, 3.14
—participating, 3.15, 3.111, 3.112
—payment by, 3.111, 3.115
—reconstruction, 3.28, 3.45, 3.74, 3.75, 3.81–3.88
—shares used, 3.36
consortium, 3.36, 3.54, 3.55
contributions, amount, 3.115
control, *see* company
corresponding shares, 3.82, 3.92
death of participant, 3.44, 3.63, 3.79, *see also* personal representatives
divestment by law, 3.47, 3.66
dividends, 3.28, 3.62, 3.75, 3.117
earnings, 3.33
eligibility for membership, 3.48–3.57
eligibility to establish, 3.14
employee-control shares, 3.42
employment, cessation, 3.44, 3.53, 3.68, *see also* death
excess shares, 3.89, 3.90, 3.92–3.96, 3.98, 3.110
full-time director or employee, 3.49
group of companies, 3.51
group scheme, 3.15, 3.16, 3.44, 3.49, 3.107, 3.111
income tax, 3.60–3.98, *see also* PAYE, Schedule E
—appropriation of shares, 3.60–3.62
—capital receipts, 3.74–3.80
—company reconstruction, 3.81–3.88
—disposal of shares, 3.63–3.73
—dividends, 3.62, 3.117
—excess shares, 3.94–3.96, 3.98
—trustees, 3.62, 3.117, 3.120
—unauthorised shares, 3.94–3.98
information
—failure to provide, 3.22, 3.125
—provision, 3.27, 3.30, 3.31, 3.120–3.124
inheritance tax, 3.119

initial market value, 3.27, 3.33, 3.67, 3.84, 3.87
investment committee rules, 3.115, 3.116
locked-in value, 3.67, 3.77, 3.84
market value, 3.27, 3.70, *see also* initial market value
material interest, 3.55, 3.56
monetary limit, 3.33
new holding, 3.82
new shares
—further issue, 3.113, 3.114, 3.116
—reconstruction, 3.82, 3.92
ordinary share capital, 3.36
other schemes, 3.54
outline, 3.1–3.13
participant
—meaning, 3.1, 3.48–3.57
—tax position, 3.58–3.110
participating company
—meaning, 3.15
—payment by, 3.111, 3.112
PAYE, 3.105–3.110
—capital receipt, 3.106
—excess shares, 3.110
—group scheme, 3.107
—participant's interest sold to trustees, 3.118
—sale proceeds, 3.106
—shares transferred to participant, 3.109
—unauthorised shares, 3.110
pensionable age, attainment, 3.44, 3.68
period of retention, 3.44, 3.45, 3.70
personal representatives, 3.31, 3.46, 3.47, 3.63
reconstruction, *see* company
records, 3.30, 3.31
release date, 3.46
relevant amount, 3.33
relevant period, 3.112
retention, period of, 3.44, 3.45, 3.70
rights issue, *see* shares
salary, 3.33
Schedule E
—assessment, 3.105
—Case I, 3.49
—Case II, 3.57
—Case III, 3.57
—long absences abroad, deduction, 3.33, 3.105
scheme
—alteration, 3.21, 3.23
—approval, 3.17–3.20, 3.23
—group, 3.15
scheme shares, 3.1, 3.36–3.43, *see also* shares
—appropriation, 3.54, 3.59–3.62
—assignment, 3.44, 3.45
—charge on, 3.44, 3.45
—company used, 3.36, 3.37
—different treatment in same class, 3.43
—disposal, permitted, 3.44–3.47
—disposal, tax implications, 3.63–3.73
—employee-control shares, 3.42
—initial market value, 3.27, 3.33, 3.67, 3.84, 3.87
—meaning, 3.1
—monetary limit, 3.33
—restrictions, 3.39–3.41
—transfer to participant, 3.46
—sale, 3.45, 3.46, 3.118
scope, 3.15
shares, *see also* company reconstruction, excess shares, new shares, scheme shares, unauthorised shares
—corresponding, 3.82, 3.92
—general offer, 3.45
—identification, 3.64
—new holding, 3.82
—rights issue, 3.29, 3.72–3.75, 3.81–3.88
stock dividend, 3.82
takeover, *see* reconstruction
trust, 3.2, *see also* trustees
trustee in bankruptcy, 3.47, 3.66
trustees, 3.25–3.32, 3.111–3.113, 3.116–3.120
—appointment, 3.25, 3.26
—dividends, 3.28, 3.117
—expenses, 3.111, 3.117
—information, provision, 3.27, 3.30, 3.31, 3.120–3.124
—PAYE, 3.106–3.110, 3.118
—records, 3.30, 3.31
—share transactions, 3.25, 3.27–3.32, 3.46, 3.47, 3.111–3.113, 3.116, 3.118
—tax liability, 3.62, 3.101, 3.102, 3.117, 3.120
unauthorised shares, 3.45, 3.89, 3.91, 3.92, 3.94–3.98, 3.110
workers' co-operative, 3.14, 3.39, 3.44, 3.46

Approved scheme, *see also* Approved profit sharing scheme, Approved selective share option scheme, Savings-related share option scheme
—pre- 27.3.74, 2.40, 2.41
Approved selective share option scheme, 1.4, 1.5, 5
advantages, 5.1, 5.3, 5.4, 5.7
alteration, 5.17, 5.21, 5.23
amalgamation, company, 5.36
approval
—alteration of scheme, 5.17, 5.21, 5.23
—appeal, 5.23
—application, 5.15, 5.16
—conditions for, 5.20, 5.24–5.49
—information, 5.15, 5.22, 5.61
—prior discussion, 5.19
—procedure, 5.15–5.23
—refusal, 5.23
—requirements, 5.20, 5.24–5.49
—withdrawal, 5.22, 5.23, 5.56, 5.58
associate, 5.45, 5.46
associated company, 5.42
capital gains tax, 5.59
cash alternative, 5.20
close company, 5.45, 5.46
company
—amalgamation, 5.36
—associated, 5.42
—close, 5.45, 5.46
—control, 5.13, 5.37, 5.38, 5.46
—control, change of, 5.36
—eligible to establish scheme, 5.12
—group, 5.13, 5.14, 5.37, 5.38
—ordinary share capital, 5.37
—participating, 5.13
—quoted, 5.38
—reconstruction, 5.36
—takeover, 5.36
—unquoted, 5.38
connected person, 5.40
consortium, 5.37, 5.45
control, company, 5.13, 5.37, 5.46
death, 5.35, 5.44, 5.54
eligibility to establish, 5.12
employee-control shares, 5.42
employment, cessation, 5.44
full-time director, 5.43
group
—of companies, 5.13, 5.14, 5.37, 5.38
—scheme, 3.16, 5.13, 5.14, 5.43
income tax, 5.50–5.58
—discount on shares, 5.50, 5.51, 5.56
—exercise of option, 5.34–5.36, 5.53, 5.56
—grant of option, 5.50
—growth in value of shares, 5.7
information
—failure to provide, 5.22, 5.62
—provision, 5.15, 5.61
material interest, 5.45–5.48
monetary limits, 5.26–5.31
option
—date of exercise, 5.34–5.36
—date of grant, 5.17, 5.18
—early exercise, 5.36, 5.54
—exercise, 5.34–5.36, 5.44, 5.53, 5.54, 5.56, 5.58, 5.59
—grant, 5.17, 5.18, 5.50, 5.51
—lapse, 5.59
—monetary limit, 5.26–5.31
—price, 5.32, 5.50
—transferability, 5.49
ordinary share capital, 5.37
outline, 5.1–5.11
participant, 5.25, 5.43–5.48
—death, 5.35, 5.44, 5.54
—full-time director, 5.43
—qualifying employee, 5.43
participating company, 5.13
personal representatives, 5.35, 5.44, 5.54
price of option, 5.32, 5.50
qualifying employee, 5.43
reconstruction, company, 5.36
rights issue, 5.32
Schedule E
—Case I, 5.58
—Case II, 5.58
—Case III, 5.58
scheme shares, 5.37–5.42
—company, 5.37
—discount, acquisition at, 5.50, 5.51, 5.56
—disposal, 5.11
—employee-control shares, 5.42
—growth in value, 5.7
—meaning, 5.25
—monetary limit, 5.26–5.31
—payment for, 5.25
—price, 5.32, 5.50
—quoted, 5.38
—restrictions, 5.39–5.41

scheme shares
—unquoted, 5.38
scope, 5.13, 5.14
share capital, variation, 5.32
shares
—bonus issue, 5.32
—rights issue, 5.32
Stock Exchange Model Code, 5.41
Association of British Insurers, Investment Committee guidelines, 7, Appendix

C

Company law, 6
directors
—loans, 6.5, 6.6
—options, 6.3, 6.4
—shares, 6.3, 6.4
employees, loans, 6.5
options, grant, 6.2
share issue, 6.2, 6.5
Comparison of approved schemes, 1.5

G

General law, 1.2, 1.3, 2.1–2.71

I

Incentive scheme, *see* Approved profit sharing scheme, Approved selective share option scheme, Savings-related share option scheme
Investment committee guidelines, 1.7, 3.115, 3.116, 7, Appendix

L

Legislation,
outline, 1.3, 1.4

N

National Association of Pension Funds, Investment Committee guidelines, 7, Appendix

O

Options, *see* Savings-related share option scheme, Approved selective share option scheme

P

Profit sharing scheme, *see* Approved profit sharing scheme

S

Savings-related share option scheme, 1.4, 1.5, 4
advantages, 4.2, 4.7, 4.8
alteration, 4.17, 4.19
amalgamation, company, 4.34
approval
—alteration of scheme, 4.17, 4.19
—appeal, 4.19
—application, 4.12, 4.13
—conditional, 4.16, 4.19
—conditions for, 4.15, 4.20–4.53
—information, 4.12, 4.63
—prior discussion, 4.14
—procedure, 4.12–4.19
—refusal, 4.19
—requirements, 4.15, 4.20–4.53
—withdrawal, 4.18, 4.19
associate, 4.50, 4.51
associated company, 4.35, 4.41
bonus date, 4.25, 4.27, 4.28
capital gains tax, 4.7, 4.57, 4.58
cash alternative, 4.15
close company, 4.50, 4.51
company
—amalgamation, 4.34
—associated, 4.35, 4.41
—close, 4.50, 4.51
—control, 4.10, 4.34, 4.35, 4.37, 4.38, 4.47, 4.49
—control, change of, 4.34
—eligible to establish scheme, 4.9
—group, *see* group
—liquidation, 4.34
—ordinary share capital, 4.37
—participating, 4.10, 4.43, 4.48
—quoted, 4.38
—reconstruction, 4.34
—unquoted, 4.38
—winding up, 4.34
connected person, 4.40
consortium, 4.37, 4.49, 4.50

control, company, 4.10, 4.34, 4.35, 4.37, 4.47, 4.49
death, 4.28, 4.53
disability, resignation, 4.31
dissenting minority shareholders, 4.34
eligibility to establish, 4.9
employee-control shares, 4.41
employment, cessation, 4.29
forfeiture of options, 4.32
full-time director or employee, 4.43, 4.44
group
—of companies, 4.47
—scheme, 3.16, 4.10, 4.11, 4.43, 4.48
income tax
—exercise of option, 4.54, 4.56, 4.59
—grant of option, 4.54, 4.59
—growth in value of shares, 4.54
—undervalue, shares acquired at, 4.55
information
—failure to provide, 4.18, 4.63
—provision, 4.12, 4.63, 4.64
injury, resignation, 4.31
material interest, 4.50, 4.51
monetary limits, 4.22
option
—date of exercise, 4.25–4.36
—early exercise, 4.34, 4.36, 4.56, 4.59
—exercise, 4.25–4.36, 4.48, 4.54, 4.56, 4.59
—forfeiture, 4.32
—grant, 4.23, 4.48, 4.49, 4.54, 4.59
—lapse, 4.36
—monetary limits, 4.22
—partial exercise, 4.36
—price, 4.16, 4.23, 4.24
—transferability, 4.53
ordinary share capital, 4.37
outline, 4.1–4.8
participant, 4.21, 4.42–4.52
—death, 4.28, 4.53
—full-time director or employee, 4.43, 4.44
—other options, grant, 4.49
—pensionable age, attainment, 4.30, 4.31
—redundancy, 4.31
—resignation, 4.29–4.35, 4.61
—retirement age, attainment, 4.30, 4.31
participating company, 4.10, 4.43, 4.48
pensionable age, attainment, 4.30, 4.31
personal representatives, 4.53
price of option, 4.16, 4.23, 4.24
reconstruction, company, 4.34
redundancy, 4.31
resignation, 4.29–4.35, 4.61
savings schemes, pre-15.11.80, 4.62
SAYE contracts, 4.21, 4.22, 4.25, 4.36, 4.60, 4.61
Schedule E
—Case I, 4.43
—Case II, 4.52
—Case III, 4.52
scheme shares, 4.37–4.41, *see also* shares
—company, 4.37
—disposal, 4.57
—employee-control shares, 4.41
—growth in value, 4.54
—meaning, 4.21
—monetary limits, 4.22
—payment, 4.21
—price, 4.23
—quoted, 4.38
—restrictions, 4.39, 4.40
—undervalue, acquisition at, 4.55
—unquoted, 4.38
scope, 4.10
share capital, alteration, 4.23
shareholders, dissenting minority, 4.34
shares, *see also* scheme shares
—bonus issue, 4.23
—general offer, 4.34
—growth in value, 4.54
—rights issue, 4.23
Stock Exchange Model Code, 4.40
Selective share option scheme, *see* Approved selective share option scheme
Share options, *see also* Approved selective share option scheme, Savings-related share option scheme
acquisition, 2.3, 2.16, *see also* grant
assignment, 2.1, 2.4, 2.5, 2.7, 2.12, 2.14, 2.20, 2.23, 2.27, 2.34
bankruptcy, 2.19, 2.30
capital gains tax, 2.23, 2.33
company used, 2.3
connected persons, 2.16, 2.21

date of grant, 2.11
director, 2.3
divestment by law, 2.19
employee, 2.3
employment, 2.6
exchange, 2.20–2.23
exercise, 2.1, 2.5, 2.7, 2.9–2.19, 2.25–2.27, 2.34
general law, 1.2, 1.3, 2.1–2.34
grant, 2.1, 2.4–2.7, 2.9–2.11, 2.16, 2.20, 2.23, 2.34
income tax, computation, 2.7, 2.8, 2.13–2.15, 2.20, 2.22
information, provision of, 2.34
instalments, payment of tax, 2.26–2.32
loss, 2.1
non-resident, 2.24
office, 2.6
payment of tax, 2.25–2.32
personal representatives, 2.10
release, 2.1, 2.5, 2.7, 2.12, 2.14, 2.20, 2.27, 2.34
Schedule E
—Cases I–III, 2.5, 2.24
—charge, 2.2–2.34
surrender, *see* release
tax, payment, 2.26–2.32
third party, 2.4, 2.16–2.18
time of grant, 2.11

Shares, *see also* Approved profit sharing schemes, Approved selective share option schemes, Savings-related share option schemes, Share options
benefit in kind, 2.68
capital growth and exceptional benefit charges, 2.35–2.62
—acquisition, 2.35–2.45, 2.51, 2.52
—assessment, 2.58
—benefit in kind, 2.35
—capital gains tax, 2.60, 2.61
—computation, capital growth charge, 2.54, 2.56–2.59
—connected persons, 2.37, 2.47, 2.55, 2.64
—director, acquisition as, 2.35, 2.36, 2.38, 2.39
—discount offer, 2.43
—emoluments, 2.35
—employee, acquisition as, 2.35, 2.36, 2.38, 2.39
—exemptions, capital growth, 2.40–2.53
—exemptions, exceptional benefit, 2.40–2.44
—information, provision, 2.62
—interest in, 2.36, 2.38, 2.54
—loan security, 2.48
—nominee, 2.38
—normal shares, 2.45
—option, 2.38
—profit sharing scheme, 2.44
—proprietor, acquisition as, 2.39
—public, offer to, 2.42, 2.43
—restrictions, shares subject to, 2.45–2.50
—Schedule E, Case I, 2.36
—Stock Exchange Model Code, 2.47
—trust beneficiary, 2.38
—unit trust, 2.53, 2.62
cheap loans, 2.63
directors and 'higher-paid' employees, 2.64–2.71
exceptional benefit charge, *see* capital growth
general law, 1.2, 1.3, 2.1, 2.2, 2.35–2.71
interest in, 2.71
loan
—cheap, 2.63
—notional interest-free, 2.64–2.68
nil paid, 2.63–2.68
partly paid, 2.63–2.68
stop loss provisions, 2.69, 2.70
'under-value', issue at, 2.64–2.68

Order form

To: Tolley Publishing Company Ltd., Tolley House, 17, Scarbrook Road, Croydon, Surrey CR0 1SQ England. Telephone: 01-686 9141

Please send me the following book(s), as shown below. I understand that if, for any reason, I am not satisfied with my order and return the book(s) in saleable condition within 21 days, Tolley will refund my money in full.

If you wish to place a standing order for any book(s) and obtain the benefits of the Tolley Subscriber Service, indicate quantity in the relevant standing order box(es). All books placed on standing order are sent post-free within the U.K. Please add 5% towards postage and packing if not placed on standing order.

Title	Price per copy	No. of copies	Standing order	Amount £
			☐	
			☐	
			☐	
			☐	
			☐	
			☐	
			Plus VAT (if applicable)	
			Plus 5% postage and packing (if applicable)	
			Total £	

My cheque is enclosed for total amount of order £________

Please debit my Access/Visa* account number

[ ] Signature________

*Please delete as necessary

Please send me a copy of the full Tolley catalogue ☐

Name†________

Firm________

Position________

Address†________

____

________ Post Code________

Telephone No________ Date________

†If paying by credit card, please enter name and address of cardholder

Registered No. 729731 England VAT No. 243 3583 67

Code 949

Tolley